IDEOLOGICAL SUBVERSION

The Radical Left's Plan to Transform America into a Socialist Police State

C. BRIAN MADDEN MEDIA, LLC.
Copyright 2019

Dedication

To God, my family, friends, and associates who continue to help make this possible.

Acknowledgement

"Mr. Trivia" David L. Strauss (1946-2018), one of the best educators that had ever lived.

Table of Contents

Chapter One: What is Marxism?

Chapter Two: Who are these People?

Marxist Men

Socially Conditioned Proletariats-The Foot Soldiers of the Revolution

Chapter Three: The Ideological Subversion of the United States of America

The Man who brought Ideological Subversion to Light

Chapter Four: Demoralization

Education

Radically Changing the Social and Cultural Environments of America

Chapter Five: Destabilization

The Economy

Law and Order/Military

Media

Chapter Six: Crisis-The American Proletariat Revolution

Civil War

Foreign Invasion

Chapter Seven: Normalization-The United Soviet States of America (USSA)

Index

Author's Notes

Introduction

Ponder this question for one second.

What if you woke up one day, and realize, that everything that you have been taught, and everything you have been told about the "evils" of the United States, was an absolute lie?

How would you answer that question?

Think about it.

As you look for an answer, let's get a brief overview about this book, **Ideological Subversion: The Radical Left's Plan to Transform America into a Socialist Police State.**

I began to write this book, because of an incident which occurred on November 7 2018, from members of the Communist Front Group, called **Antifa**.

The Washington D.C. wing of ANTIFA, called **Smash Racism DC**, led by Marxist Revolutionary Mike Issacson, attempted a home invasion of the residence of Fox News Channel Talk Show Host and Conservative-Republican **Tucker Carlson**.[1,2]

The group, numbering approximately 20, attempted to violently cause physical harm and property damage to the Carlson home that day, resulting in hundreds of thousands of dollars in property damage. Fortunately, most of the Tucker and most of his family was not home at the time.

However, as Issacson and his band of hooded and masked anarchists smashed windows of the Carlson home and property. As they were causing severe damage to private property, they were spray painting the Antifa symbol on the walls of the residence, shouting **"No Borders, No Walls, No U.S.A. at all!"**.

And the purpose of their actions?

To quiet all opposition to the Communist Order, via threats and intimidation, and to fundamentally transform the United States into a Socialist hellhole like Venezuela. All in accordance with Karl Marx and Friedrich Engels' ***Communist Manifesto***.

It is just that simple.

I also tackled this topic in my books ***Don't Believe the Hype!! (First Revision)*** and ***The Big Black Lie by Little Red Commies*** **(the latter, soon to be published)**.

Ideological Subversion reinforces the deadly doctrine called **Marxism**, and further explains why there appears to be so much hatred and division in this country as of late.

Because such anger, hatred and divisiveness are caused by Marxists on purpose, with the explicit intent on destroying the United States of America from within.

Marxists in both positions of governmental power, and inside every level of society have been brainwashed over the years, some by birth, that the age-old art of Man having differencing opinions concerning the current socio-economic climate of the time, has now become a thing of the past.

At a time where the concept of **Conservatism**, the love of the socio-economic system of the United States as founded, with limited government and representation by the people, used to differ from the ideology of **Liberalism**; where the love for this country was still apparent, but social issues and bigger government is looked upon as the problem solvers. In this day and age, such differences has now become one-sided.[3,4]

Liberals are now no longer Liberals of the past.

In 21st Century America, **Liberals** have now become **Marxists**, the deadly ideology of **Karl Marx** to destroy the entire economic and social system of the United States at all costs; even if it means that innocent lives are lost in the process![5]

Those who have a different opinion against Liberals and Marxists in the country, are now targeted on purpose as opposing the latter's twisted view of the world; and those who they call "dissenters" need to be eliminated altogether, via discreditation of their works, character assassination through the media and physical violence.

Hence, the reason why Tucker Carlson and his family were specifically targeted, by irrational people, like Issacson and his merry group of violent and brainwashed anarchists.

Groups like Smash Racism D.C. and dozens of splinter groups like them, carryout numerous protests, violent actions and what is called **"Agitation Campaigns"**, for one major purpose; to control every aspect of human activity in American Society.

What economic and social system does that very thing? **Socialism** first, then **Full-Communism** last.

These Communist Front Groups, are staffed by, paid for and operated by Marxists and their psychologically weak-minded Dupes, known as **Liberals**. Or what one Russian Dictator, Vladimir Lenin called the latter, **"Useful Idiots"**.[6,7,8]

So, why is it important for the reader know this?

Because, one must fully comprehend and understand, that Marxists in power, under the cloak of "Equality", "Civil Rights", and "Fairness", have been trying for over 100 years, is to essentially transform the United States and remaking the country in the image of the old Soviet Union and the current Socialist countries like Cuba, Venezuela and North Korea.

Places where the people were or are subjected to injustice, harsh punishment, and enslavement, where nothing is equal and freedom to do what you want does not exist!

The reason why I chose the title of this book is to educate the masses of people, who still do not understand why our country, the United States, is under attack from both outside forces like the UN and within or borders, Marxists and their Liberal Dupes, right in your face.

The title of the book within itself, *Ideological Subversion: The Radical Left's Plan to Transform America into a Socialist Police State* will give you the reader, the knowledge into understanding as to how the

Radical Left's actions, which are done on a daily basis, is part of a scripted plan of action, with the main goal of creating a classless, stateless society.

The same classless, stateless society, which Karl Marx and Friedrich Engels have advocated in the 19th Century; where **Vladimir Lenin, Joseph Stalin, Mao Zedong, Ho Chi Minh** and others implemented in the 20th Century; now **American Communists, such as Barack Obama, Nancy Pelosi, Hillary Clinton, Valarie Jarrett, Bill Gates and many others** want to create the same society in the 21st Century.

A Utopia of sorts, where everybody and everything is perfect.[9]

Where no diseases exist, no God exist, where everybody lives and work for the whole of communities and not for their individual selves. A false Utopia, where no laws, rules and regulation exist to tell you what you can do and hold you accountable for your actions.

A Utopia where no families exist as a unit, because everybody and every child and women will belong to whole communities, instead of each other!

A place where no one will own property, and each produces in accordance "with one's need", where universal peace and universal prosperity will exist.

However, unless you are in Heaven, for Man to improve the lives of others, via individual thinking, innovation and the means/will to succeed, a perfect Utopian World never will exist ever on Earth!

It is a pipe dream!

Yet, Marxists want to convince you that such a Utopian World did exist at one time in human history.

They have been led to falsely believe, that a Utopian world should once again occur again in the "future". However, there are **two main obstacles** that are hampering their efforts to transform the United States into a Socialist State; the economic system called Capitalism/Americanism and the American people who supports it.

In their twisted view of non-reality, both obstacles must be **eliminated** in the process, in-order to bring about a perfect world, where everybody will be equal.

None of this stuff is made up!

Since the 2016 Presidential Election between Multi-Billionaire Real Estate Tycoon and Reality Television Star **Donald J. Trump** defeated in a landslide three-time Presidential Candidate, former Secretary of State and First Lady **Hillary Clinton,** now-President Donald Trump, who has by-the-way, been duly elected by the people of the United States, as the 45th President, have been in a constant battle with the Marxists in power for a number of years. Of course, none of these Marxists who occupy positions of political, financial and governmental power, are no fans of President Trump and are not fans of the people who elected him to power!

In their brainwashed minds, since their plans of destroying the United States of America from within are now in jeopardy, Marxists are no longer hiding as to who they are and what they believe in.

As a matter of fact, one could look at the Presidential Elections of the 44th President of the United States, **Barack Hussein Obama** in 2008 and 2012 respectfully, has given the Marxists in power some sort-of "Green Light", to advertise their plan for destroying the U.S. and taking over the world to implement their classless, stateless society.[10]

In the meantime, these same Marxists will continue to push their Marxist agenda, continually implemented in four basic stages, called **Ideological Subversion**, in-which this book will explain in detail what it is and how it's affecting the United States as we speak.

Secondly, inside the next Ideological Subversion Series, which will be published in the future, the reader will gain a full comprehensive understanding into how the American Left, along with their Useful Idiotic Duped Liberals, will constantly recycle and re-brand these areas as something new, which there isn't anything new about them.

Their goals are still the same; to destroy the United States of America from within!

After reading this book, if you the reader, are not scared or concerned about that is happening right now, at this very moment, then nothing will scare you, when the iron boot come crashing down on to your neck!

If the Marxists Tyrannical Leaders has successfully transformed the United States into a Soviet-like country, there will be no other place where to run to![11]

If we allow the evil Marxists takeover the country of the United States and implement their form of Socialism, then;

Your freedom of Religion, Freedom of Speech, Freedom of the Press, the Right to Private Property Ownership and the Freedom to purchase and own a gun to protect your family and your property, will no longer exist.

Then what?

You will no longer be living in a free society, because the United States of America, as it was founded, will no longer exist as a sovereign nation!

You will then live in **Tyranny**.

Think this will not happen here in America? It certainly can!

And it is being done, right now at this very instance, by those who harbor evil intentions into destroying this beautiful and wonderful country, called the United States of America! To bring about "change" and to implement their deadly version of Marxism here on American soil, Communists will fight to end of their very own existence to succeed in doing so, **only if you the reader allow them to succeed**!

C. Brian Madden

Southern Missouri

March 22, 2019

Chapter One: What is Marxism?

In short, the Communists everywhere support every revolutionary movement against existing social conditions. Let the ruling class tremble at a Communist Revolution. The Proletarians have nothing to lose but their chains, they have a world to win. Working men of all countries, unite!"

~Karl Marx~[1]

So, the reader may ask this one fundamental question; what is **Marxism**?

Why should the reader be concern about it?

Marxism (also called **Communism**), is the political, economic and social principles or policies, materialized into an ideological doctrine by it's founders **Karl Marx** (1818-1883) and **Friedrich Engels** (1820-1895).[2][3]

In-essence, Marxism is a deadly ideology, which teaches that evils of the World, in the form of Crimes, Poverty and Disease, are caused by the economic system called **Capitalism** (also called **Americanism**).

Marxism teaches their followers, that the economic and social[4][5][6] engine of Capitalism, are operated by a collective few individuals, called **Bourgeoisie**, who are wealthy land and factory owners who has exploited the Working Class, called **Proletariats**' labor, to enrich themselves.

Marx and Engels stated in their book ***The Communist Manifesto*** written in 1848, that the **Bourgeoisie** earn huge profits by selling manufactured goods on the open market. The goods which they sell, are assembled by the low-waged factory worker (**Proletariat**) in hot, busy, and unsanitary factory conditions, who do not receive none of the profits of goods being sold.

As a result, the Proletariat live in squalor living and social conditions or in abject poverty, while the Bourgeoisie live in pristine mansions.

Marx and Engels further theorized, that the latter has become so selfish to keep their wealth, that the Bourgeoise put into place a series of institutions, laws and religion, to prevent the Proletariat for sharing in the Bourgeoisies' wealth, causing economic and social inequities.

To eliminate the distinction between the two after-mentioned classes of people, the Proletariat shall rise-up in rebellion and destroy the Bourgeoisie in an all-out violent and bloody revolution.[7][8]

By doing so, the Proletariats themselves takeover the economic production of society, produce goods and services in abundance, sell them on the open market, and thus, shall share the profits made from the sales among themselves.

Marxism teaches, that once the Proletariat overthrow and destroy Capitalism, among those destroyed, the **Bourgeoisie** and any other dissenters who doesn't accept the former view of the World, then all social and economic inequity will be eliminated around the World by each country, when they rise-up in a Revolution.

At the same time, when the Capitalistic society is eliminated, disease and poverty will also be obliterated, therefore the Proletariat can start to build a New World Order (NWO) of **universal peace**, and **universal prosperity**. A New World where Man would be truly equal, both economically and socially.

A Utopian World on Earth.

In other words, the Proletariats shall establish for themselves not just a One-World Utopia, but everyone in this new society will produce goods, services and collect the profits from the sales of such things, not for themselves, but for the **whole of the community**. Therefore, no one will become wealthier than another, everything will be *Ceteris Paribus*; all things remain equal and unchanged.[9][10]

Marx and Engels theorized, that in-order for the Proletariats to rise-up against the Bourgeoisie in a worldwide, violent revolution, a **Communist Order** must be established first, which will serve as the blueprint for such revolution to take place.

In 1847, the men created the **Six Principles (or goals) for the International Communist Movement**;[11][12]

> *To Overthrow Capitalism*
>
> *The Abolition of Private Property (Ownership)*
>
> *The Elimination of the Family as a social unit*
>
> *The Abolition of all Economic Classes*
>
> *The Overthrow of all Governments*
>
> **The establishment of the Communist Order, with Communal ownership of property in a Classless, Stateless Society.**

One must understand, that if the Communist Movement becomes successful, in this Utopian world which Marx and Engels had theorized, there will be no borders, no distinction between town and city, no distinction between state and country, no laws, rules or regulations for people to abide by. The type of the World where morality, when it comes to knowing what is right and what is wrong, does not exist; **nothing**.

In other words, a society of total equality.

A society which is rich in anarchy, where the people themselves, will commit genocide among each other!

People who believe in the doctrine of Marxism, are called **_Marxists_**.

In the United States of America, the job of Marxists is to destroy Capitalism/Americanism and replace it with **Socialism** first, and **Full Communism** (the Utopian World) last.

So, what is the difference between Socialism and Full Communism?

The difference between Socialism and Full Communism is this; **Socialism believes in a One-World Government, which will control all aspects of human activity, once Capitalism/Americanism is destroyed.** In Full Communism which will come after the One-World Government has "whiter away" on its own, **no government will exist, and all human activity will be controlled by the society-as-a-whole.**

Those who advocates for Socialism are called **Socialists**, and of course, those who believe in Full Communism are called **Communists**. Both are labeled by the public as Communists! No matter what term are used, either Socialists or Communists, they both believe in the **ideology of Marxism**, therefore they should be called *__Marxists__*!

So, who are these Marxists? Let us find out.

Chapter Two: Who are these people?

The creators of modern-day Marxism, Karl Marx (left) and Friedrich Engels (right). (Courtesy of Wikimedia Foundation)

Karl Marx and Friedrich Engels knew, that for their plan of Full Communism to take shape, a new breed of Human Beings must be psychologically conditioned to carry out the Marxist mission, for worldwide domination.[1]

They are called **_Marxist Men_**, which encompasses all genders, races, nationalities, and cultures. All which are found right here, in the United States of America.

***The objective of Marxist Man, at the end, is to force society into Socialism first, then Full Communism last. Whether society like it or not.*[2]**

To explain who and what Marxist Man is, and expose their plan to achieve world domination, the reader must objectively understand from the get-go, that the mindset of such persons is **_extremely dangerous_**.

This selected group of people have been specifically chosen by other Marxist Men and Women, to further carry out the destruction of America, in accordance with Karl Marx and Friedrich Engels' writings.

However, Marxism has since been modified, one way or another by other former followers of Marxism, who ended up being domineering dictators of their respective countries, such as[3,4]

Vladimir Lenin (1870-1924)-Soviet Union/Russia

Joseph Stalin (1878-1953)-Soviet Union/Russia

Nikita Khrushchev (1894-1971)-Soviet Union/Russia

Mao Zedong (1893-1976)-People's Republic of China

Pol Pot (1925-1998)-Cambodia

Fidel Castro (1926-2016)-Cuba

Kim Il-Sung (1912-1994)-North Korea

Ho Chi Minh (1890-1969)-Vietnam

Patrice Lumumba (1925-1961)-Congo

Maurice Bishop (1944-1983)-Granada

Idi Amin (1923-2003)-Uganda

There are many others, which are too numerous to list in this publication.

Saul Alinsky (left), George Soros, Valerie Jarrett (center), Barack Obama and Hillary Clinton (below).

(Courtesy of Wikimedia Foundation)

Marxist Man is a conditioned criminal.[5]

They are persons who have been psychologically brainwashed, usually from their parents, grandparents or by someone who they are very intimate with. These brainwashed people are taught to reject what they see and only react, to specific verbal stimuli from their masters who controls them.

However, for this psychological transformation to occur, some retooling of their reasoning must be accomplished first.

This is to keep them focused in-order to react to their master's every beck and call. Marxist Men are programmed to outright reject all dependency on free will, ethics, morals, to include their inability to think to rationalize for themselves, regardless whether-or-not, true information is right in front of their face.[6]

This Marxist Man concept is not new to human history.

Many power-hungry people in the past, have had this kind of dream that one day, ***they*** would be the ones, who can dominate the World and create their own version of a perfect Utopia, here on Earth. Historical figures include **Nimrod, the Son of Cush** and Great-Grandson of Noah was the first person to invent the idea of Marxist Man to exist.

Greek Philosopher **Plato** (428 B.C.-347 B.C.) wrote about such a utopic world in his book "***Republic***", while **Saint-Simon the Zealot** advocated for it. **Karl Marx** and **Friedrich Engels**, succeeded by materializing Marxist Man into physical existence.[7]

Now, let us explore ***how*** Marxist Man is conditioned to be a psychopathic-conditioned criminal.

On the outside, Marxist Man seems to appear rational in thought and behavior, highly intelligent to those who either work with him or see them in the public. However, this a deceptive tactic, because those who have mentally subverted to become Marxist Men, have reduced his or her thinking to the lowest common denominator.

This is a ruse.

In-reality, Marxist Men are slick, cunning, and conniving creatures, who are snobbish, selfish individuals who decisions are highly predictable for those who can see right through their think-skinned deception. They are devoid soul and repudiates their capacity for immortality.

They believe that there is no universal Creator!

Marxist Men have accepted the notion, they were "***accidents***" of Nature, so they have ***no morals***, approaches all issues directly, and will flat out deny that such radical behavior is not his or her fault. When such situations or narratives ends up failing because of their actions, Marxists will deny that it was their fault. They will begin to blame others for their failure, calling them "***stupid***", "***ignorant***" and accuse such distractors of harboring "***self-motives***" against them.

These conditioned criminals believe that the world revolves around them, and not the other way around, which is why Marxists have a constant thirst for more and more power. Their objective is to take over larger and even larger populations of Men, Women and Children, which is why they have a serious appetite for control.

Remember, their mission is to dominate the World.

Marxists perceive themselves as being "*special*" and have been placed into society to conquer Nature, the Universe, and all senses of reality. The latter part, reality, they have been taught to control, where they themselves write the narrative (story) and sell it as something real, which is not.

The idea behind this deed, is to formulate a paranoia-type atmosphere, project superiority over everyone else, with the criminal intent of creating mass chaos.

Marxist Men feels that they are superior to everyone, regardless who close or how distant of the relationship others have, who associates with them. They perceive themselves as the "**Kings and Queens of the Jungle**"!

Marxist Men are usually found in positions of power in political, financial, business and academic areas of American society. They are not shy or even care about who they really are. This includes what others think about them or how they portray themselves to the outside world.

The only thing they understand is destroy Capitalism/Americanism, destroy the family, divide people by race, culture, sexual orientation, and their own nation's sovereignty!

They will believe this objective regardless or not they personally benefit from the very same economic system that they are trying to destroy!

Marxism It is a hate mentality.[8, 9]

Marxist Man venomously despises the Military and its members of Active Duty Servicemen, Women and Veterans, because they perceived such people as a threat to their false sense of superiority and world domination. He or she envisions a small body of people who have been criminally-conditioned like themselves who has the power to legislate, adjudicate and operate via **The United Nations** as "**The State**" to take charge of the World prior to implementation of Full Communism.[10,11]

Once Marxist Men are created in enough quantity, they are driven by their creators to teach others, who they feel are weak-minded individuals, to think like they do.

Who do you think they target the most?

People who are on the low-income economic scale, those who have low self-esteem about themselves, alcoholics, drug abusers, drug dealers, the Elderly, the Young, criminal gang members and organizations, inner-city people, regardless of skin color; people who sometimes don't live in-reality by themselves!

Marxist Men target those who are very susceptible, to accept what is told to them as being factual, without verifying whether such information is true or not. They understand that such easily manipulated people, will become their advocates or "Proletariats" in their quest to destroy Americanism. [12, 13]

By doing this, the people become "_useful idiots_", to be used as verbal tools and support Marxist Man's agenda to implement Socialism and full Communism here in America.

Marxist Man's psychological subversion have also extended to even those who are members of some of the most innovative generations in the United States to date, such as the last portion of the **"X"-Generation, the Millennial Generation** and the **"Z"-Generation/Post-9/11 Generation** of American people.[14, 15, 16]

However, Marxist Men will brainwash younger people of America, to accept Socialism/Communism subliminally, to control their actions, emotions, and responses to the former's made-up narratives. By doing so, the young will be-seen-as the "**Proletariats**" or the "**Foot Soldiers of the Revolution**" and they will be instrumental into the fundamental transformation of the United States of America.

These subverted population of young Americans, will be transformed by Marxist Men into **Socially-Conditioned Proletariats**, who will attend Communist/Socialist political rallies, take to social media and advocate for Socialism, demonstrate and conduct anarchical violence against those who Marxist Men have trained them to hate. Their target are Conservative Americans and others who are going against the Communist Order.

Socially-Conditioned Proletariats-The Foot Soldiers of the Revolution

Many of you readers have not heard the term "***Duped Liberals***".

One may ask, who are and why is it important for us to know who they are?

Because Duped Liberals are just as dangerous, if not even more dangerous than Marxist Men themselves.

Duped Liberals are also inflicted with a Social mental disorder called **Narcissistic Personality Disorder**, or **Narcissistic Psychopathic Disorder; NPD for short.**[17, 18, 19]

Yet, in this chapter, we will explore who the Duped Liberals are and describe their behavior, which is similar in scope with Marxist Men. The exception being that the former is considered the *"Foot Soldiers of the soon-to-be Revolution".* The main idea of subverting Liberals into accepting Socialism first, then Full-Communism last, is to have an army of millions of people, to proclaim that they are the victims of Capitalism/Americanism.

Once they, the Duped Liberals believe in the lies and deception which Marxist Men have labeled them as being victims of their own circumstance in the United States, these same Liberals will begin to act out their rage and hatred towards this country and everybody who continue to support it.

In other words, Marxist Men want a core of millions of American people, to exploit and use them to "***take the fight into the streets***" or "***to mobilize***" sacrifice themselves, including their lives, in the name of "Equality", "Fairness", "Civil Rights" and "The Cause".

To bring the country into Crisis.

Democrat House of Representatives Alexandria Ocasio-Cortez (left), Ilhan Omar (center) and Rashida Tlaib (right). (Courtesy Wikimedia Foundation).

Regardless, persons who are inflicted with Narcissism are dangerous, because they can serve as, what Vladimir Lenin once-termed "**useful idiots**". Why? Because, they can be easily "duped" or suckered into believing whatever Marxism Men tells them to be true, regardless whether the information is true or not, persons afflicted with NPD will follow willingly **without question**.

It's just like leading a bunch of Lemmings, over a cliff for self-destruction.

Duped Liberals form the core of Socialism/Communism because they have been led to believe, falsely of course, that their circumstances in life is a direct result of Capitalism, and not through any fault of their own. Since they are the victims of an "**unjust**", "**unfair**", "**racist**", "**bigoted**" and "**homophobic**" society, Marxist Men in power and influence will label these groups of people as the Proletariats.[20, 21]

Therefore, since these Duped Liberals have accepted the lies of Marxists and their propaganda machine as being victims and Proletariats, it will be their job to sacrifice themselves for the so-called upcoming "Revolution" in America.

Understand, Liberals who have been duped by Marxists *really believe what they are told and will defend it at all costs!*

These after-mentioned hoodwinked people are not only are found in America's Inner-City communities, by they can be found in wealthy, affluent neighborhoods and/or cities located throughout the United States.

Unfortunately, in recent times, Foreign-born populations, who have both legally and illegally immigrated to the United States, have taken up the torch to proclaim they are victims of Americanism!

Persons born in Central America, Southeast Asia, the Middle East and African countries, have fallen prey to becoming the biggest and most numerous pawns in the game of "equality" that Marxists in America has falsely portrayed.[22, 23]

Since Marxist Man sees such people as weak-minded individuals, such persons can be found in abundance in places of higher learning, such as Public Schools, Community Colleges and even inside major Universities across America.

One must clearly understand and remember, that **Marxist Men despises and look down on such easily manipulated people**!

To keep the after-mentioned people subjected to them and only to them, Propagandists will use other specific words or phrases to make it clear, without hesitation, that they are using these people, to further their agenda to destroy the U.S.. Because they have been brainwashed to accept that this country, the United States of America, was founded unjustly and harbor absolute contempt towards.

Such phrases like <u>***"Persons of Color"***</u>, when referencing Minorities, or "<u>***White Privilege***</u>" is just one out of many examples, which Marxist Man uses to keep such persons subjected to them, while simultaneously demeaning those who they have absolute control over.

People afflicted with Narcissistic Personality/ Psychopathic Disorder (NPD), are categorized with a long-standing sense of Grandiose, either in fantasy or in real, everyday behavior. Narcissists are inflicted with an overwhelming need for admiration and have a complete lack of compassion or empathy for others.

Duped Liberals who have this condition truly believe that <u>***they***</u> are the primary importance in everybody's life and whoever they meet. At the same time, such person often display a snobbish, self-loathing attitude, while they exaggerate their achievements, talents and often claims to be superior in intellect or "logic". Even though, these persons don't have a clue about anything they speak of having such logic.

Photo of Duped Liberals chanting for Vermont Senator and Communist, Bernie Sanders at a rally, early 2019. (Courtesy of the New York Post)

    Narcissists often speak badly behind the backs of their family members and friends, by putting them down in conversations that they themselves are the 'clearer thinkers'. Anybody who Duped Liberals feel superior to, when it comes to public opinion or during a discussion of something substantive, such as politics or social issues, must explain to **_them_**, why you think the way. Concurrently, Liberals will not offer any explanation of their views, to counter-balance your view of the topic of discussion whatsoever![24, 25, 26]

    They fell they don't have-to, because they have been led, falsely, to believe that they are better than you! They have been brainwashed to think they are **the smartest people in the world**, when their actions prove otherwise!

    Duped Liberals are often preoccupied with fantasies of unlimited success, power, beauty or ideal love about themselves.

    Just like Marxist Men, they consider themselves "special", "the chosen ones" and the only type of people who can understand them, are those who are just like them, mentally.

    However, underneath that false sense of self-superiority, Narcissistic people have a very low Self-Esteem about themselves, which is why they always seek out admiration from others. They always need others to praise them for their made-up superiority.

This makes them perfect targets for Marxist Men to use because the latter will constantly coddle the former by constantly giving praise and admiration to persons who will support their devious plan to transform America.

Duped Liberals afflicted with Narcissism, have a strong sense of self-entitlement, expect favorable treatment and/or automatic compliance with their demands for everyone, regardless whether their expectations are unrealistic or difficult to attain.

As for empathy for other people's feelings, Narcissists could care less about that!

They are exploitive of others, take advantage of everyone else's work or success and claim it as their own. Narcissists are rife with jealousy and envious of others, even though on the surface, they will discredit such accusations against them. While in the next breath, they then twist the accusation around to make it appear like **_you are jealous of them!_** [27, 28, 29]

Narcissists are **_arrogant people_**, and if anybody questions their fake sense of grandiose and mental superiority, they will be called nasty names, such as '**stupid**', '**evil**', '**mean**' and '**too dumb**' to recognize their '**brilliance**'. Remember, they could care less if such words demean the people who they target with such insults. Understand that by doing so, they receive personal satisfaction because they have been subverted to think they are superior to you!

They are sick mentally and are physical wrecks, who act differently in public than in a private setting, which is why Narcissistic people have-to put up their false façade.

They feel that they deserve more than they have already accumulated, as they dream of winning big cash prizes without doing any work to achieve it, who at the same time, perceive themselves as absolute perfect Human Beings who are flawless in Nature! Because of this made-up false sense of self-superiority, they will adamantly deny that they are the ones who can never do anything wrong; it is everybody else's fault, not theirs!

When such Narcissistic people are exposed that they were wrong in their decisions, discussions, or in their actions by others, all they will do is deny it.

When denials don't work, they will start lying and when lying fails, they began to blame others, again.

If blaming others doesn't work, then they will launch themselves into a tyrannical rage, consisting of jumbled words, phrases, and vulgar language, which doesn't make sense and accusatory in nature.

To those who are not Narcissistic, these actions further show how mentally unstable that the useful idiots of Duped Liberals really are. Many will react and direct their sense of self-superiority into physical confrontations or criminal actions to prove to those doubting them, who they say they are; superior, unblemished figures.

They are truly, dangerous people!

Using lies, deception, and manipulation to achieve their goals, they will exploit others in such fashion to gain the upper advantage of those who they feel superior to. Narcissistic people, whether they are Marxist Men or Duped Liberals, regularly provoke others to fight, then end up losing the fight and blaming the provocation of the fight on others!

Narcissistic people are not grateful to those who they seek help from and will take all the credit for the idea at the end, claiming as such *'it was my idea in the first place'* when it wasn't.[30, 31, 32]

As for criticism, Narcissists hate it!!

Any criticism, whether constructive or not, will send these people into a rage and will respond with foul-mouth words meant to critically demean the criticizers. They will do so, to the point where they will short-fuse themselves and appear psychotic. One must clearly understand, that people afflicted with NPD, cannot fend for themselves because they think the world revolves around them!

Marxist Men love Duped Liberals, because they want Narcissistic people who act-like and are mentally inept just like them, because they can easily be duped to help do their dirty work, to destroy the current society.

Finally, in-order for the Communist Revolution to transpire, the dismantling of Americanism, such actions must be done and accelerated, methodically, through a slow process called ***Ideological Subversion***.

Chapter Three: Ideological Subversion of the United States of America

"...Subversion in Soviet terminology is always an aid and to destroy the country, nation or geographical area of your enemy."

~Yuri Bezmenov~[1]

Ideological Subversion, also called **Psychological Subversion**, or simply "Brainwashing", is the act of manipulating large populations of people, to believe in false information. The intent of Ideological Subversion by Marxists, is to change the perception of reality of the American public, using deceptive tactics, to control the targeted population's emotions and actions.

The way Ideological Subversion works, is by using the country's mass communication system, so that propagandists, who dress themselves up as **"Journalists"** or **"Experts"** can instill lies, deception and the twisting of factual-information, to control the targeted population's reaction to a certain, manufactured situation. By doing so, propagandists can change the perception of reality of the American Public's to such an extent, that no one can come to any sensible conclusion as to what is really fact or what is fiction.[2, 3, 4]

The goal for these mentally deranged Marxists is, that by changing the public's perception of reality, by repeating such lies on a continuing basis, the people will eventually accept, without question, that lies are believed as factual information.

Joseph Goebbels, Adolf Hitler's Minister of Propaganda during the 1930s and 1940s sums up Ideological Subversion of a population as such;

"If you tell a lie big enough and keep repeating it, people will eventually come to believe it, and you will even come to believe it yourself." [5,6]

So, by lying to the public on a consistent basis, while constantly rebranding the lies over again and present it as something new, even though it is just the same argument, people will begin to believe that such lies are basically true. What they want is when people become fed up of being lying to each and every day, they will just simply "give up" and submit to the powers that be, all aspects of their freedom of speech, choice and opportunity to fundamentally transform the United States into another Soviet Union.

In the process of constantly lying in the face of the American people, the propagandists will eventually come to believe their own lies as well. Remember, their objective is to destroy Capitalism/Americanism and the United States of America, the last bastion of freedom, to instill Socialism first, then Full Communism last.

Lying to the public is also the goal of Marxists in their effort to force the American people to accept Marxism as the savior of the world's ills.[7, 8]

Some sources credit the actual term of Ideological Subversion to Susan Hadley, who was the lead member of the late-1970s and early-80s Cyberpunks criminal organization. Her group consisted of computer hackers, who were known to infiltrate Federal Government and U.S. Banking systems databases to illicit information.

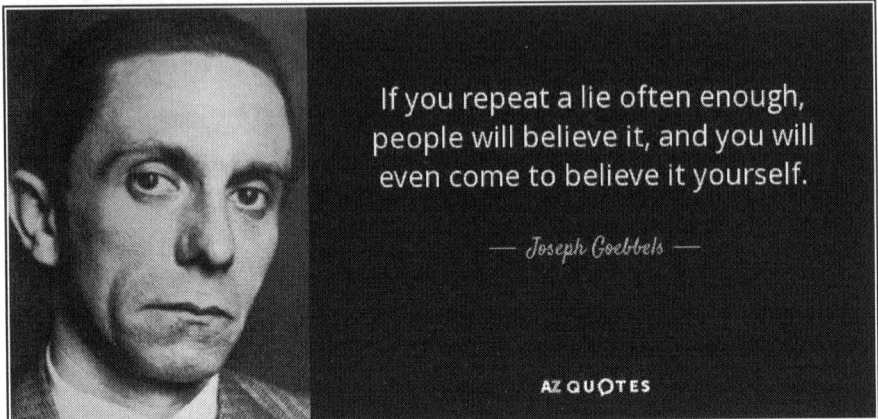

> If you repeat a lie often enough, people will believe it, and you will even come to believe it yourself.
>
> — Joseph Goebbels

However, the term Ideological Subversion/Psychological Subversion was coined by the Soviet Union KGB propaganda machine, long before Hadley was born in 1959.

The Soviets under the dictatorship of Joseph Stalin (1878-1953) and later under Nikita Khrushchev (1894-1971), used the term **"Active Measures" or aktnbhble mepbl**, to describe their system of changing the Western nations population to overthrow Capitalism.[9, 10]

One of the many men, who have brought such an evil scheme to light, was the former KGB Defector **Yuri Bezmenov** (1939-1993).

The Man who Brought Ideological Subversion to Light

Yuri Alexandravich Bezmenov, also known as Thomas Schuman, was born in 1939 in Russia to a high-ranking Soviet military officer and Communist Party member. At the age of 17, he was educated in the Moscow State University, which was directly controlled by the Soviet Intelligence Service (KGB) and the Communist Party Central Committee, where he studied Oriental languages. In addition, Yuri Bezmenov studied History, Literature and Indian Culture.

After graduation, he was drafted to take military training, where Bezmenov learned how to plan military operations, using maps of foreign countries and how to interrogate Prisoners of War (POW).

Soon after his military training was complete, Yuri was sent to India in 1963, where he worked as a Russian Translator and Public Information Officer (PIO). Two years later, he was recalled to Moscow and began to work for **Ria Novosti** Magazine's Government Political Publications Department (GPPD), where he wrote Marxist propaganda pieces as a Journalist to Western newspapers.

Many of his editorials were published in large American Newspapers and Magazines, such as the **New York Times**, **Washington Post**, **USA Today** and **Time Magazine** to name a few.

Yuri Bezmenov along with his fellow GPPD co-workers, who were also trained by the KGB, conducted Potemkin Progressive-type tours as hosts, to Westerners who visited India to learn about the so-called joys of Socialism.[11, 12]

Mr. Yuri Alexandervich Bezmenov (known as Tomas Schuman).

(The Author's Collection)

During these fake, staged events, propagandists like himself, intentionally manipulated these visitors into accepting Socialism as "the new way forward of human progress", if their home countries will implement it.

These Duped Intellectuals, Business Leaders, Government Officials and members of the Religious Clergy did that very thing; returned home and began to sing the praises of Marxism to their respective populations.

Bezmenov, after working for **Ria Novosti** Magazine, became sickened with the economic system of Socialism in both India and Russia. His feelings turned to abject hate for the Socialist economic system, when he found out that many of his co-workers and friends who worked with him was targeted by the Soviet KGB for "**Liquidation**" (by murder). Apparently, the Russian Intelligence Service were conducting surveillance on Bezmenov and his fellow propagandists, making sure that they did continue to promote the glories of Marxism in their editorials or while touring with their Western dupes.[13, 14]

By 1969, Yuri Bezmenov decided to defect his post in India and the Soviet Union for good. In February 1970, Yuri succeeded in defecting from his post, by camouflaging himself as a visiting American Hippie, who were sent abroad to place like India to learn that country's culture.

Once out of India, he fled to Athens Greece, where he was debriefed by U.S. Intelligence Officials, and was granted asylum in Canada, under **Prime Minister Pierre "Pete" Trudeau** (father of Canada's current Prime Minister, Justin Trudeau).

After working various jobs in Montreal Canada, he was hired by the Canadian Broadcasting Corporation (CBC), using the name Thomas Schuman.

In 1979, Pierre Trudeau pressured CBC executives to fire Bezmenov, because the latter's broadcasts condemning Marxism was becoming too effective to the average Canadian listener. That year, feeling the pressure from the Prime Minister, Soviet President Leonid Brezhnev and the KGB, the CBC fired Yuri Bezmenov. [15]

In 1980, he fled to the United States and from that time until his death in 1993 in Toronto Canada, Yuri Bezmenov lectured at American Universities across the nation, like the University of California-Los Angeles (UCLA), Stanford University, the University of Georgia and many others.

It was during these lectures, Bezmenov introduced to the American Public the evils of Marxism and lectured students on college campuses, U.S. Military Intelligence organizations and Federal Government Officials about the dangers of Ideological Subversion. Persons who was brainwashed into accepting Socialism by guys like himself, who have brought back to the United States singing the "equality" of Socialism for decades. He did television interviews, including one with John Birch Society member and television political documenter **G. Edward Griffin** in 1984.

While living in Los Angeles during the 1980s, Yuri Bezmenov was the author of four well-renowned books;

Love Letter to America (1984)

No Novosti is Good News (1985)

Black is Beautiful, Communism is Not (1986)

World Thought Police (1986)

Even though Bezmenov was only one of many popular Soviet Union KGB defectors, such as **Oleg Kalugin (1937-1995)** and **Viktor Andreyevich Kravchenko (1905-1966)**, Yuri's description of Ideological Subversion is considered the best. [16, 17]

After all, he was an expert at what he did, while serving as a Soviet Propagandist while working in India for ***Ria Novosti*** magazine!

While lecturing in some of America's Universities, Yuri Bezmenov describes the **Four Stages of Ideological Subversion**, where Marxists both in America and from around the World who have targeted (and continue to do so) the United States of America, as founded, for utter destruction.

When Bezmenov lectured at the University of California-Los Angeles (UCLA) in 1981, he readily admitted that the United States of America was already conducting Ideological subversive techniques on American Citizens, orchestrated by the **Soviet Secret Service** (the KGB, now called the **Federal Security Service** (FSS)).

Dispelling the rumor that the Kremlin, in Moscow, that the KGB at the time were using spies to carry out their subversive activities unsuspecting Americans, Bezmenov stated that the time and money spent by the Russians on espionage operations on U.S. soil took only 15% of their total budget.

The other 85% of the KGB's budget was allotted to slowly brainwash the American Citizens to accept Socialism instead of Capitalism, via the media and education systems was divided into **four basic stages**; [18, 19]

Demoralization

Destabilization

Crisis

Normalization

However ideological subversion of American citizens has been taken place, in one form or another, since at least the 1850s.

Yet, it has only been 120-plus years on American soil, starting in the 1890s, where there been a concerted effort, along with a constant push to destroy Capitalism within various populations within the United States to radically change its political and economic structure. Soviet Propagandists, however, has specifically targeted following people of major influence, since at least the 1920s, to conduct their own subversive activities on the American public; [20, 21, 22]

Hollywood Actors, Actresses

Music and Entertainment Industries

Journalists of Newspapers, TV Networks and Magazines

American Diplomats

Foreign Exchange Students

Artists and Sculptors

Business and Chambers of Commerce

Academia and Educators on all levels

Civil Rights Leaders and Organizations

Religious Clergy

Politicians, Judges and Lawmakers on every level of government

The key in Ideological Subversion, according to Yuri Bezmenov and other KGB defectors, is a two-way Street. A person, a community, a society or a country **<u>cannot</u>** be brainwashed to accept Marxism, if such entities **<u>does not want</u>** to be subverted to accept such a doctrine.

A great illustration of this can be seen in the country of Japan, between the 13th and 19th Centuries.

Japan began to open their society, a little bit at a time after United States Navy Commodore **Matthew C. Perry (1794-1858)** visited the island nation 1853. Prior to this meeting, Japan was pretty much a closed society. Perry's orders were the established diplomatic and trade relations between them in the United States.

Other nations around the World, prior to Commodore Perry's visit, have tried and fail to convince the Japanese Diet to open their society up to them. These countries were told politely to either leave them alone, outright rejected other nations interference into their culture and Geo-political system, or in the case of China or Russia, went to war with these countries.

One must understand, that the only way a person, population of people, or a country can be subverted to accept Marxist-Leninist Principles, is if the targeted country responds with openness to the entity targeting them.

However, between 1851 and 1905, America only been lukewarm in accepting Marxist-Leninists principles. In-reality, the spreading or Marxism took off during the Russian Revolution, conducted between 1917 and 1918, when Russian Czar Nicholas II and his family was murdered by the Bolsheviks, which brought Vladimir Lenin to power. This event and upon the establishment of the **Communist Party of the United States of America (CPUSA)** in Chicago in 1919, is when in the United States have had enough subverted Communists, to ramp up operations of Psychological/Ideological Subversion on its own people. [23, 24, 25]

The act of brainwashing your adversary's population is nothing new to him in history. Over 2500 years ago the Chinese Philosopher **Sun Tzu** (544 B.C.-496 B.C.) wrote about a tactic, in which the Chinese Warriors could use to destroy the enemy, without shedding one drop of blood;

"To implement state policy an award like manner, it becomes inefficient to fight on the battlefield. So, if you want to successfully implement your States' policy, is not to fight at all. You must subvert your enemy for a-period-of-time to such an extent, where he does not see you as the enemy, but will accept you as your civilization, your ambitions and like your enemy as an alternative."[26]

In 21st century America, the teachings of Marxism using Psychological Subversion reaches almost **every aspect** of the American culture. This radical perversion is being taught right now in Political, History and English Classes on every level of the U.S. Public School System and at all three US Military Service Academies as well as **every college campus nationwide**.

Ideological Subversion requires that a new type of human being be produced, in lieu of the continuing brainwashing of American citizens by generation. For the subversion to be successful you have-to create least two-separate entities, who will be the ones that are tasked to not only conduct the intentional brainwashing of Americans, but to keep such subversion going on and pumped into the soft heads each successive generations of American Youth. The two-separate entities are called;

Marxist Men

Duped Liberals

Using these labels interchangeably, both require criminally-conditioned Marxists to create a slow, 20-plus year process to tear down any, and all rational thinking of the population. By doing so, those who will end up accepting the doctrine of Communism, will eventually fall for the lies and deception, to the point where they cannot rationally think for themselves. Once they achieve that level of subversion, the latter will begin to feel emotionally bad of their country, and to verbally or physically act out in a delusional rage, that they, society made them victims of their circumstances. Not because of their own incompetence, as mentioned in the last chapter.

Sun Tzu, author of The Art of War and founder of Ideological Subversion. (Courtesy of The Fifth Field.com)

Marxist Men will blatantly lie and deceive the weak-minded people, that their conditions and/or environment will never change, because of some **"outside forces"** that are lined against them, in which cannot be controlled.

Examples of such outside forces, who Marxist Man uses to make this argument, are a person's skin color, the inherited traits that they received from their parents, which they will pump into the soft brains of weak-minded people, that these forces will never make them "*productive citizens*".

Marxist Men consistently tell these people, that they are the ones who understand their "plight" and they will be the ones who will lead the weak-minded people, who they called "victims of oppression" to revolt against any or all opposition to the Communist Order. [27, 28]

Marxist Men will be the people who will fight and defend the poor, the downtrodden, the drug dealer, the Elderly, the Felons and those who haven't **"had a fair shake in life"**, when they won't. As a matter of fact, once Marxist Men have successfully conditioned these the aforementioned people into do their bidding, they are taught to manipulate the same people into doing the dirty work for Marxists for "***The Cause***" of "***Freedom***" and "***Equality***".

Code words that tends to keep such mentally-subverted people, subjected to the conditions which they have been reduced to.[29]

Also, such weak-minded persons, in Marxist Man's world view, must stay subjected to them and only **_them_**, even if it means paying their supporters who they have manipulated, money and benefits in the form called "**_government entitlements_**" to keep them subjected and controlled.

Chapter Four: Demoralization

Demoralization is the process, where individuals in a society is brainwashed to no longer believe in themselves, in their families, in their communities, or their country.[1]

To demoralize and country, such as the United States, it would take 15 to 20-plus-years to subvert one generation of Americans to accept Marxism and reject Capitalism.

Why so long?

Because it would take that much time to completely change the reality of one generation of US citizens, before another generation can begin the process of Demoralization. Understand, that this process is ongoing and is continuous, regardless of the political climate of the country at the time or whoever is President during that moment.

Yuri Bezmenov in a television interview with G. Edward Griffin in 1984, that at the time in America, the demoralization of American Citizens was being "over done". He further explained that by 1984, Marxism was being taught by Marxist Men to other Marxist Men and Liberal Dupes, to such an extent, where such subversive activities have reached such critical areas in society and government, that it will be **_almost impossible to change course_**.[2]

Demoralization (15 to 20 Years)		
IDEAS		
1. Religion	Politicize, Commercialize, Entertainment	Death Wish
2. Education	Permissiveness, Relativity	Ignorance
3. Media	Monopolize, Manipulate, Discredit, Non-Issues	Uninformed Myopia
4. Culture	False Heroes and Role Models	Addictive Fads, 'Mass'
STRUCTURE		
1. Law and Order	Legislative, Not Moral	Mistrust 'Justice'
2. Social Relations	Rights Vs. Obligations	Less Individual Response
3. Security	Intelligence, Police, Military	Defencelessness
4. Internal Politics	Party, Antagonisms	Disunity
5. Foreign	Salt... Friends	Isolation
LIFE		
1. Family, Society	Break Up	No Loyalty (State)
2. Health	Sports, Medicare (NHS), Junk Food	Enfeebled Masses
3. Race	Lower the Uppers, Bible Genetics Vs. Environment	Hatred, Division
4. Population	De-Land, Urbanize	Alienation
5. Labor	Unions Vs. Society	Victimization

The first mass generational subversion of teaching Marxist Ideology took place, immediately at end of World War II. Those born are called the **"Baby Boom" Generation** of Americans, where a enormous increase of newborns increased the population between the years 1946 and 1966. This generation was the first group of American youths, who were subject to brainwashing. This was conducted by both Soviet Union KGB agents, Russian propagandists, and those American citizens in high level-society who were already Marxist propagandists themselves. The latter were called '**Potemkin Progressives**'.[3, 4, 5]

Both Soviet KGB agents and Potemkin Progressives used the Media/Educational-complex, to teach and subliminally subvert, millions of Baby Boomers to reject Capitalism. Of course, those ones doing the subverting have been falsely led to believe, that the United States of America, from its founding, have been the cause of all the evil in the world because of its so-called racist past against minorities.

Understand that most of the U.S. Baby Boomer Generation, were born and raised during the American Civil Rights Movement, where Marxist Propagandists specifically targeted to teach such Marxist garbage, on TV and inside the classrooms across the nation.

So, accepting Socialism or what is now called "**Globalism**", interchangeably, finally the United States can be a fair and just society, under the fake mantra of "**Social Justice for All**"

During the Demoralization process, propagandists target specific areas in this country to actively subvert and change the perception of millions of people via these following organizations.

Religion/Churches

Education/Schools

Media

Culture

Law and Order

Social Relations

Security

Internal Polices

Foreign Relations

Family and Society

Healthcare

Race Relations

Population/Land Ownership

Big Labor (Unions vs. Society-at-large)

In simpler terms, the Demoralization process teaches the younger members of the population to hate everything and anything American. They are taught that the Founding Fathers were Aristocrats, rich White Men, who wielded enormous power, who did not care about the actual people who made them rich.

Sounds familiar?

The younger generation are also taught that any failures in their lives are **not the fault of their own but is society's fault instead**. Soviet propagandists and their Potemkin Progressive minions, have also taught the young that whatever they do in life, "**the odds are always stacked against you**" and that "**you would never have any equality, or amount to anything because the color of your skin**", when leveling such demonic accusations to minorities; or "**Persons of Color**".

During the Demoralization process, propagandists would also teach the younger generation that those who occupied positions of authority, such as **Law Enforcement Officers**, **Teachers**, **Parents** or **Grandparents**, don't care about them and should be ignored altogether. That they should challenge these people directly and reject their authority outright.

Marxists will further brainwash the younger population, in-particular Minorities, to think that **no one has authority over them** and that law enforcement officers are racist "*__Pigs__*", who hate minorities and will kill you because the color of your skin, especially when it comes to White Officers.[6,7,8]

Remember, it is a mental game that Communists and Socialists play on the young population.

It is at this point when out of nowhere, large "movements" are artificially created and publicize for all to see.

Movements such as the **Nonviolent Movement, Black Power (Black Panthers), Anti-Vietnam Protestors, Weather Underground, Symbionese Liberation Army (SLA), American Indian Movements (AIM)**, and more formed within the American Civil Rights Era of the 1950s and 60s.

Of course, Marxist Men always attempt to rebrand something as being new or "grassroots", when this is far from the truth.

Groups such as **NOW! La Raza (The Race), Female Liberation Organizations, Lesbian-Gay-Transvestite-Queer or (LBGTQ), Black Lives Matter (BLM), Occupy Wall Street (OWS), Organizing for America (OFA), ANTIFA** and the **#Me Too Movements** in the present-day, have become politically and socially relevant.

These movements, and many other Communist front groups, are all manned and operated by trained Marxist propagandists, to include their Duped Liberal and Useful Idiot followers, will enhance the demoralization process, by making those who have been subverted to accept Marxism to portray themselves as the new victims of their own circumstances.

And Americanism is the cause of their problems.

The after-mentioned movements are also financed by a host of philanthropy foundations, which are assisting the demoralization of America, like Wall Street Hedge fund, multi-billionaire George Soros and sons **Open Borders Society Foundation**, the **Milton S. Eisenhower Foundation**, the **Ford Foundation** the **Borealis Foundation, and** the **Bill & Melinda Gates Foundation** to name a few.

Yuri Bezmenov has stated that.

*"**The Demoralization process is complete in America**."*

He also stated that the process was "over done". Since the American Baby Boomer Generation was the first mass generation to undergo subversion to accept Marxism, millions of these people who are now adults have been brainwashed to the point where;

<u>*"They have been contaminated and can not be changed back into reality."*</u>[9]

One must understand that the same Baby Boomer Generation of Marxists, as of this writing, are currently occupying seats in within the Federal Government!

They previously served or currently serve as elected Congressmen, Congresswomen, U.S. Senators, appointed Civil Service Executive Agencies and Judicial Branch of government. Many of them, were once Civil Rights Activists, Communist Party of America (CPUSA) members and Communist Front Group Movement members, who were raised during the 1950s and 1960s. Some were even subverted during the 1970s and 80s, who were a part of the X-Generation of Americans.

Ponder that for second.

In the meantime, let us dig deeper into how the Demoralization process have subverted (or perverted) specific areas of American culture.

Religion

One of the first areas of Marxist "action" is to destroy the Institute of Religion.

One must be reminded, that religion dictates the higher power, God, via his Messenger, Jesus Christ identifies the differences between what is right and what is wrong.

Karl Marx who was a raving Atheist lunatic, wrote in the Communist Manifesto that.

***"My objective in life is to dethrone God and destroy Capitalism."*[10]**

The Marxist Theory of Religion not only rejects it outright, especially Christianity and Judaism, but he wrote that any religion **was not of divine origin but are manmade myths or fallacies**. In other words, Marx considered that the Institute of Religion is used by the Bourgeoisie (the Dominant Classes) to suppress the Proletariat (the Exploited Classes).

In addition, Marx and Engels also considered Religion was purposely created by the Bourgeoisie, to teach the poor their roles and duties in maintaining the former rights of private property ownership, in which in their view, the latter didn't own themselves.

Both Marx and Engels wrote, that in-order to create a perfect Utopian peace within the world, Religion must be destroyed, because it was an appendage of the Capitalistic society.

So, the task of the Marxist propaganda machine in America, is to replace Religion with either No Religious beliefs, discredit God as a made-up human being who has no power over people whatsoever and replace it with Man as Supreme Being of the Universe, instead of God.[11,12]

The second task of propagandists in America, in their effort to destroy Religion as part of the American Culture is to replace Religion with.

Sex Cults

Scientology Cults

Jehovah Witnesses

Polygamy Communes

Pedophilia Cults and Communes

Christianity Cults (where the church leader is considered God)

Radical Islamic Beliefs and organizations

One must not forget that Marxism teaches its listeners that in-order to create a classless, stateless society, the current society of Capitalism/Americanism must be done away completely.

Again, the distinction of "what's good" and "what's bad", including all belief in morality, must be fully and totally obliterated in the American Culture!

In simpler terms Marxist propagandists in America have been and continue to teach successive young generations that,[13,14]

The Bible is a myth

Man created God, and not the other way around

Remove any references to God from the Courthouses, Houses of Congress and in Schools across America

Substitute Psychology for Religion

Deify Science

Create the conditions where Priests, Pastors, Bishops and Nuns will commit sin within the church, and conduct sexual-perverted acts with children

Make the Birth of Jesus Christ (Christmas) about Alcohol, Drugs and Material things

Make the Resurrection of Jesus Christ (Easter) about an Egg and a Rabbit

Accept that you must love yourself more, than loving others

Replace Religious organizations with Hate Organizations, such as Satanic Cults, Churches or Fraternal Organizations

Education

This second step into Demoralization process is the teaching a Marxist Ideology in the American Public-School Curriculum.

At this stage, Marxist propagandists working as College Professors, High School Teachers, Elementary School Educators, are no longer teaching students the basics of Math, English, Grammar, History, Writing, or Science. In its place, a new radical Marxist ideological driven curriculum is created.

The basic school curriculum will be replaced by subjects such as.

History of Urban Warfare

Natural Foods

Earth Science

Climate Change

Sexuality

Educators would teach students about "**Calorie Counts**", while encouraging them to consume of more **organic foods**, sold with questionable sanitation practices and **less processed foods** which the propagandas will say, **causes obesity and other major health problems**. They would teach the younger generation that **Genetically Modified Foods (GMOs)** should be avoided all together. No more teaching elementary students of **The Five Basic Food Groups**, such as bread, vegetables, fruit, milk and dairy products, and lean meats.

Remember, for Marxist Men to create their Proletarian Army-like Foot Soldiers of the Revolution, the aforementioned students are taught not to critically think for themselves! They must obey their masters, who are brainwashing them on TV, Social Media and of course, in the classrooms to parrot the Communist line, to further push the agenda of "Equality".

Communist Professors and Educators will teach **Earth Science** and the lie that manmade **Climate Change/Global Warming** to their students.

These Duped Liberals will present false computer models, made-up data charts and create indoctrination videos, to back up their claims, that Man himself, in the United States, of course, is responsible for the "Pollution" and "Dirty Air/Water" which plagues the Planet. They will present this Climate Change as something real, to the point where the liars will brainwash children, teens and even adults, that if something is not done about Climate Change "right away", that we will all die in a matter of years![15,16,17]

To extend this delusional hysteria of Climate Change, the after-mentioned Professors and Educators, will emotionally hype up such "doomsday scenario" of that the Earth is on the verge of dying very soon, is due in-part of man's progress due to Capitalism/Americanism.

This lie will be constantly reinforced on Television, in Music, on Social Media, that if Man (meaning the United States) does not change course as soon as possible and prevent the Polar Ice Caps from melting, or reduce C02 emissions to **"Net-Zero"** by 2050, we will all die in some form of natural disaster or pandemic event!

Congresswoman Alexandria Ocasio-Cortez at press conference regarding her proposed plan for a Green New Deal, addressing the Climate Change hoax.

(Courtesy of the Elder Stateman)

Marxists and their Duped Liberals will have instilled fear of impending doom into the young minds of America, and as such will end up believing what they are told as being factual.

This is dangerous.

Of course, none of the latter is true, but during the Demoralization stage, just the fear of the world "dying off" before they reach full adulthood, will override any critical thinking skills or common-sense reasoning that they, the young generation, have left.

Each succession of newer generation of Americans will thus become "**Earth Activists**", "**Environmental Activists**" or "**Climate Change Activists**". They have been subverted to rebel, sometimes violently, against those who they see as "**Climate Change Deniers**" or those who don't believe in "**Environmental Justice**". Some Duped Liberals have even gone so far to openly call for the so-called Climate Change Deniers **to be publicly executed by murder in cold blood**, for the latter's denials that Climate Change is real![18,19,20]

You can not make any of this up!

This is who they are.

As far as traditional grammar words, these will be replaced with new words, with convoluted spellings and non-sense meanings, which will further program students to confuse them and destroy any other rationality that they have-to comprehend facts.

For example, children used to be taught, when learning Grammar and Handwriting, to print letters of the alphabet, combine words and phrases, then learn the art of using *Cursive Writing*.

Cursive Writing is a style of penmanship, in which some characters which are written, are joined in a flowing manner, with the purpose of writing faster. This skill was once taught in Elementary School, between 3rd and 5th grades. However, since the late-1990s and early 2000s, Marxist Educators have altogether thrown out the curriculum of Cursive Writing, without any explanation.

Ever wondered why?

Cursive Writing requires consistent, repetitive practice which will fine tune a child's motor skills, dexterity with precise movement control, and increase their brain activity. This form of writing will also enhance that person's visual and tactile abilities, needed later-on in life. Many experts have explicitly stated that Cursive Writing, requires concentration and rational thinking skills. Skills required to further and enhance one's multisensory experiences. By doing so, bring into being one's thoughts and ideas at a much faster in an organized fashion, especially when it comes to creative writing conducted by hand, as compared with a keyboard.[21,22]

This explains why Marxist Men dropped the curriculum altogether; because they can not allow children to rationalize and think for themselves, while being creative, because the former cannot control their actions.

Remember, the whole idea of Ideological subversion, is to "dumb-down" the population, so that during the Demoralization phase, the young can be exposed-to and accept Marxist principles, to fundamentally transform America into a Socialist system.

Because as a child develops and become teenagers and finally adults, if they could rationally think for themselves, then they can eventually figure out the evil and diabolical plan that Marxists have for this country.

This should never have happened, yet it has.

Now States throughout America, is not only junking the Marxist education curriculum, such as **Common Core Math**, which is only half of the entire **Common Core Curriculum Standard**, but States are now introducing legislation that reintroduce the penmanship of Cursive Writing as well.

As of 2016, 14 States have reintroduced Cursive Writing as mandatory curriculum in their schools, while starting in the Fall of the same year, the largest Public-School System in the nation, New York City, has reinstituted the curriculum in their schools. By January 2018, the number of states that had dropped the Common Core Standard swelled to 18. Four states, Virginia, Texas, Nebraska, and Minnesota never adopted Common Core Standards in their schools.[23,24]

One thing Marxists in positions of power and prestige does well; they never give up their chances to rename, rebrand and reinstitute their agenda. Unless we, as the American people continue to stand up against them, the United States of America as it was founded will not survive and Karl Marx's dream of a perfect Utopia, which has only led to death and destruction will come true.

Radically Changing the Social and Cultural Environments of America

The Italian Communist Party leader (PCI) and Father of Marxist Culture, **Antonio Gramsci** (1891-1937) once stated.

"I give Culture this meaning: exercise of thought, acquisition of general ideas, habit of connecting causes and effects...I believe that it means thinking well, where ever one thinks, and therefore acting well, wherever one does."[25,26]

What Gramsci was trying to say is that one can radically change the course of your community, society, and country by creating general ideas on how to destroy the basics institutions of America, by transforming is culture for all to accept, whether they like it or not!

The following paragraph have-to be repeated.

Understand the goal are Marxist Propagandists in all levels of American Society, is to change the composition and structure of the U.S. Geo-Political system. To successfully do that, Communists must also change the American Culture of Patriotism and love for one's family, community, and country, and turn it into the culture that will readily accept Marxism instead.

In Demoralization, the traditional institution of the country such as marriage family and loyalty organizations are replaced with fake organizations such as the **LBGTQ**, **#Me Too!** and **Black Lives Matter** movements instead.

Once you have taken away the initiative of people and naturally establish responsibilities, then place them with artificial bureaucratically control bodies, then promote the latter as changing the cultural landscape of America, then you will have forcefully transformed the American Culture without any push back.

Instead or social neighborhood programs, like **Crime Watch** or **Neighborhood Watch Programs**, replace the later community institutions with **Homeowners Associations (HOA)**. HOAs bills themselves as the "**protector of property owners rights**".[27]

As a matter of fact, HOAs have significant legal power over property owners inside their jurisdiction.

Homeowner Association have Board of Directors and a President who are duly elected to enforce and oversee the HOA's governing documents.

Residents before moving into houses, apartments or condominiums located inside such HOA communities, must sign what is called a **Covenants, Conditions and Restrictions (CC&Rs)** Contract prior to move in. CC&Rs set in writing, that list certain rules and restrictions that property owners can or cannot do on or inside the homes on HOA property.

Conditions include the type of landscaping or fences allowed, selection of paint and colors a resident's house must have, the number of cars which a resident can have parked on the street or in their driveway at any given time, the size or length of a Flag pole, if it is authorized by the HOA governance. The CC&Rs include fines and penalties, with optional litigation processes if the rules in the CC&R are violated.

Once all the terms are agreed upon between the HOA and the resident, property owners have-to pay a fee to live in the community called **HOA Fees**.

With the after-mentioned being said, HOA's, rules, regulation and enforcement are all created by whom? The employees who are employed by the Homeowner Association. No. This is all dictated by the bureaucratic bodies above them, and who are they? The State in which the HOA property is located.

Does the above seems like freedom to own property and land as dictated by God or does it sound like the suppression of property ownership and freedom to do what you want to on your own land as dictated by bureaucrats?

You decide.

Another way that the Demoralization process is instrumental in destroying the traditional American Culture, is to replace social interaction with one another, with **Social Media platforms**.

The traditional way of communicating between person-to-person, either in a group one-on-one, causing face-to-face interaction, Communists has now replaced such human interaction by Social Media platforms like **Facebook**, **Email**, **Instagram**, **Twitter** or **Snapchat.**

Social media platforms are particularly relevant today, because such technology has fundamentally torn down the basic human instinct of face-to-face social interaction with other people. In many cases, Social Media has caused many people to lose any but all ability to communicate directly, either with their thoughts or ideas (or personal troubles) with each other, on-a-daily basis.

Thanks to Capitalism/Americanism, along with our innovative creativity, to improve our standards of life, owned by individuals at the beginning, has turned Social Media platforms into technological giants, often termed as **Silicon Valley**, so called for their central location near San Francisco California.

However, Social Media has become a double-edge sword to the American Culture and to the destruction of sacred institutions of America.

Major Social Media platforms, such as **Facebook**, **Google-Plus** and **Twitter**, has been instrumental for Marxist propagandists to fill these online media entities with lies, distortions of the truth.

College Professors, Liberal Duped Activists and even Marxist Politicians, have used Social Media as a tool, in their attempt to silence any and all opposition to their Communist agenda. Many of the after-mentioned people, have created many fake profiles on Social Media, in their effort to target Conservative-Republicans to either be "shadow banned" the latter's profiles, or be placed in "Facebook Jail" for long periods of time, without any rational explanation whatsoever! Some of these Social Media giants have gone as far as to permanently deactivating the latter Social Media accounts!

These same College Professors, Marxist Activists and Duped Liberals, have targeted businesses, advertisers of Conservative Radio and Television Hosts with bad publicity, in their effort to destroy their businesses or public reputation!

Social Media has even mobilized thousands of other subverted Liberals to cause anarchic insurrection on our streets and against our own citizens. These platforms in addition, have been instrumental in their efforts to silence any and all opposition of those individuals who are against the Communist Order, to include death threats or actual physical bodily harm or homicide.

One person in-particular in recent years, who have become a major target of the Marxist Propaganda machine, is the world-renowned Libertarian Alex Jones.

Alex Jones, who operates **Info Wars**, in 2018, have come on constant attack by Marxists in high-levels of society, to the point where they have banned all Info Wars broadcasting, podcasts and even permanently took down his videos on You Tube, to send a message to anybody else who Marxists feel are a threat to their plans for world domination.[28,29]

Other Radio and TV personalities who are outspoken critics of Liberal Dupes and the Marxist Propaganda machine, that have had hostile attacks against their personalities and companies using Social Media, are **Rush Limbaugh, Sean Hannity, Tucker Carlson, Michelle Malkin, Candance Owens** and many more, are constantly painted as targets by Communist Activists on Social Media Platforms to silence of their views, using techniques, such as "**Shadow Banning**", "**Facebook Jail**" or other Stalinist tactics in their efforts to shut people up.

This author has received the same overt treatment on Social Media, as well.

However, such attacks have been silenced by yours truly, using the Left's own tactics against them!

Yet, we will always fight back against the Communists and Socialists who are trying to remake the United States of America into another Venezuelan, Cuban, North Korean or Soviet Union hellhole!

In his outstanding book, former FBI Agent and bestselling Author of **The Naked Communist**, the late **Cleon W. Skousen** (1913-2006), listed what he called ***the* 45 Goals of Communism**. It was inside this first book, where he lists and describes the plans for the Marxists in America overthrow of the United States, in a violent and bloody revolution.

Inside his book, Skousen illustrates how Communism/Socialism will fundamentally change the American Culture, which further supports Antonio Gramsci's "Cause and Effect" argument, to destroy us from within;[30,31,32,33]

Promote the United Nations (UN) as the only hope for mankind

Resist any attempt to outlaw the Communist Party

Use technical decisions of the Courts to weaken basic American Institutions by claiming their actions violate a selected population's "Civil Rights"

Gain control of the schools and use them as transmission belts for Socialism and Marxist Propaganda. Soften the curriculum and take control over Teachers Associations, while simultaneously rewrite textbooks to tote the Communist Party's line of "Equality", "Civil Rights", "Human Rights" and "Global Sustainability".

Change historical events when teaching of American History, by discrediting such incidents as being only minor issues within the "big picture" of society in general.

Continue discrediting American culture by degrading all forms are artistic expression, by eliminating all good sculptures, educational and historical statutes from the public parks and buildings. Substitute artistic expression with shapeless, awkward, and meaningless forms.

Eliminate all laws governing obscenity by calling them "censorship" and a violation of Free Speech and Free Press.

Breakdown cultural standards of morality by promoting pornography and obscenity in books, magazines, movies, radio and television.

Present homosexuality, degeneracy, and promiscuity as "normal natural and healthy".

Discredit the American constitution but calling it inadequate, old fashion, out of step with modern needs, and is a hindrance to effect "social change" worldwide.

Discredit their American Founding Fathers, by presenting them as selfish Aristocrats, a bunch of racists, who had no concern for the "common man".

Support <u>any and all social movements</u> and give them centralized control of all educational institutions (i.e. Social Security Administration, States' Social Welfare Programs) and Mental Health Clinics.

Emphasize the need to raise children away from the negative influence of parents.

Eliminate the need for children to grow up in two-parent households.

Attribute prejudices, mental blocks or health and learning disabilities of children to the suppressive influence of parents.

Create the illusion that violence, racism, sexism, slavery and insurrection all legitimate aspects of the American tradition.

Pervert the American culture, by advocating for Same-Sex Marriage, Same-Sex Parenting, Polygamy, Childhood Marriage, Child

Sexual Abuse, and questioning whether-or-not <u>the gender of a child can only be determined by society and not biologically</u>.

Erosion of America's Political and Social Power Structure

In the Demoralization phase of Ideological Subversion, the traditional way in which a country like the United States, is form via the electoral process, by the nations' people at large, will be considered as being "unfair" and "unjust".

Marxists and their Duped Useful Idiots called Liberals, will advocate for a better political and social power structure, which will be "just" in their view, would be decided by the **leaders of society and not the people**! They will also push for the abolition of the Electoral College, which determines Presidential Elections, and favor of the Popular Vote, instead.

By doing so, in which the Founding Fathers had envisioned that such an idea was going to happen inside this country in the future, so they created the Second Amendment of the U.S. Constitution; to prevent a hostile and non-friendly overpowered government.

A hostile overreaching and over oppressing government which, in their view back in the 18th Century, would one day takeover the United States.

Instead of the President of the United States being the representative of all the people of the United States, Communists only want large population centers, such as Los Angeles, New York City or States such as California, New York or Texas, to have the power to determine who will be in charge other country, at the latter's approval.

Yes, Marxists are just that evil.

The next question would be, who will be leading the call to erode United States Political and Social Power Structure this way?

<u>The Mainstream Media.</u>

<u>**The American Media apparatus, during the Demoralization phase of Ideological Subversion, would be given enormous amount of monolithic power over the citizens, to the point where such non-elected people, who have no clue about reality and who are not too-smart at all,**</u>

will have control over every aspect of your mind, over every decision you make in life, and control what you should believe in or not believe in.

How does the unelected media acquire the power to decide what is good or what is bad, against you the people and the President of the United States of America (Donald J. Trump) and his administration?

In the words of the late Maryland Governor and Vice President of the United States, **Spiro T. Agnew** (1918-1996) stated this to answer the question;[34]

"[The Media] are a bunch of snobs."

They are.

The Marxist Un-Elected Media, are filled with Left-Wing Activists, are one of the many entities who uses Ideological Subversion to push millions of Americans and to accepting Socialism, while at the same time they are destroying Americanism.

The following news outlets and their affiliates, are all filled with Marxists and their Duped Liberal Useful Idiots;

Cable News Network (CNN)

Microsoft National Broadcasting Company (MSNBC)

American Broadcasting Company (ABC)

Columbia Broadcasting System (CBS)

National Broadcasting Company (NBC)

Public Broadcasting System (PBS)

Black Entertainment Television (BET)

Oprah Winfrey Network (OWN)

Arts and Entertainment Network (A&E Network)

Univision (UNI)

Al Jazeera-America

British Broadcasting Company-America (BBC-America)

New York Times (NYT)

Washington Post (WaPo)

Los Angeles Time (LATIMES)

USA Today

San Francisco Chronicle (SF Cron)

The Huffington Post (Huffpo)

These organizations and many like them, are operated by so-called "Journalists", who have been programmed to think that they know everything, when in-reality, they don't know anything.

There was once a time in America, when the news used to be the news, and when these Journalists reported the news, it was up to you to form your own opinion, to rationalize what have been reported. That is no longer applicable in 21st Century America, it will be the media, which will not only about or make-up what has happened and increase the incident 100x more than what it is, but will tell you what to think, and how you should interpret the news they report to you.

Again, these unelected unknown "Journalists" are Marxist Activists, whose job is to push lies untruths and deceptions down the throat of the American people. Their sole purpose is to manipulate the population's rationality of events, to the point where they control the outcome of emotions inside the said population.

In countries like the United States, the country's power and political structure is slowly, but methodically, being eroded away by Marxists is who don't have the qualifications, nor the will of the People to keep them in power; **but yet they do have unfettered unchallenged monolithic power over you.**

Law and Order

During Demoralization of a nation like the United States, the systematic structure to protect American Citizens using Law Enforcement agencies are being eroded away slowly.[35]

A great example of this can be illustrated by the way Hollywood and Television programming change the public's perception a law enforcement officers during the late 20th century.

Back then, television programs such as **Adam 12 (1968-1975)**, **Starsky and Hutch (1975-1979)**, **Hawaii 5-0 (1968-1980)** and many others, portrayed the image of Law Enforcement Officers with high regard, in the public's eye. Police officers, Detectives, Lawyers and even Judges, were looked upon as heroes of society, especially by elementary children, as fighters of crime to make our streets safe. Commercials like **Mc Gruff the Crime Dog**, Cartoons like **Superman, Batman and Robin, Underdog** and countless of other examples taught people from around the nation, that "crime doesn't pay."

Fast forward to the late 1980s and early 1990s and even now 2019.

Law Enforcement Personnel today, are look down upon by half the nation's population, as being ignorant, dumb, angry, and psychotic. Police are called derogatory names like, **"Pigs"**, who often abuse their power and projected superiority up on the people, especially when it comes to dealing with Minorities like Blacks and Hispanics.

Officers are often spit up on, violently beaten up, killed in cold-blood and yes even ambushed using small arm fire and bombs, because of their **"racist past"** and the murdering of **"innocent Black Men by the thousands each day"**. Lies put out by the psychotic Marxist Propagandized Media, reinforced daily by the Hollywood Elites, Entertainers and half-baked activist Journalists, to include crooked Politicians in the

Democrat/Communist Party and **the 44th President of the United States himself, the Community Organizer, Barack Hussein Obama!**[36]

Motion pictures and Television shows today portray <u>**Criminals**</u> as being heroes of society, regardless whether their actions are fueled by dangerous mental illnesses, illicit drugs such as Fentanyl, Heroin, Bath Salts, Cocaine, Marijuana or Methamphetamines.

During Demoralization of America, the Criminal takes the place of Law Enforcement Officers, as heroes to the youth in America, who they now look up to, as guidance to live their lives!

These so-called "loving Criminal" is portray by Marxist Propagandists, many of the ladder, are criminals themselves, is doing crimes by fighting an "in-just" American society, that has Enslaved Blacks, created Jim Crow Laws and treat the poor like dirt. The Media shows, that it is society's fault and is the blame for their oppressive conditions which they have been reduced-to! It is Capitalism/Americanism who gets the blame for his or her Devious actions.[37,38]

It's not the Criminal's fault, or the Gang-Banger's fault.

<u>**You are at fault**</u>, because people like you protect America and its racist past, is why the criminals are rebelling against society.

<u>**It is your fault**</u>!

At least, that's what the Communist and Socialists in America want you to accept!

It's an absolute lie and many of them know this!

Again, many Propagandists believe their own lies too, **we must not forget that!**

This hatred image is also directed towards the US military, when it come to the law and order.

Generals and High-Ranking Officers, Enlisted Men and Women on Active Duty, to include the two-million-plus population of Military Veterans, are labeled as **"warmongers"**, **"baby killers"**, **"who have waged** meaningless wars overseas" "to push the American Way of Life down the throats of innocent people".

Never mind the fact, that the same people who the U.S. Military had in the past, in the present and in the future, are the ***real people*** who are being tremendously oppressed, jailed unjustly without Due Process, and killed by brutal dictators by the thousands!

Real people that live in Third World countries who truly live in squalid conditions. Living conditions that are so extreme, that when compared to the poorest American living in the streets, the latter seems rich and glamorous when measured equally to each other.

The main goal of Ideological Subversion during the Demoralization process in the United States of America, is to sew hatred, mistrust and absolute contempt towards any written or enforced law and order, which protects its citizens.

Marxist Men and their subverted Liberal Dupes will instill into the soft brains of our youth, that such rules and regulations, to include those people who support them, are the true oppressors of society, who keep the low-income "**People of Color**", oppressed-as-a-whole.

Law and Order, in the eyes of the criminal, is looked upon as a set of rules to further establish moral principles of good and bad, which are now seen as immoral, oppressive and is put into place to protect the "**White man's money**", and the "**White man's country**".

It must be understood, that Karl Marx himself, wrote in the Communist Manifesto, and during many of his newspaper editorials, that laws are put into place, to protect the Bourgeoisie from the Proletariat, stealing his so-called ill-gotten riches.

Younger generation or being taught this lot each day and it is sickening!

Labor Relations

Here, the communication lines between Employer and Employee is constantly being eroded and destroyed.[39]

The natural established order between parties of individuals, bargaining with each of other over better pay, better benefits and better work hours and conditions, have now been changed to the point where Marxist-Leninism exchange of goods are now accepted.

Using the illustrations below, **Party A has five sacks Grain and Party B have five pair of shoes**, that they want to trade among each other. Since both want what each other has in their possession, each party will negotiate with each other, to come up with an agreement, so that each will exchange their goods among each other.

The bargaining process is complete.

This is called "**The Natural Exchange of Goods and Services**".

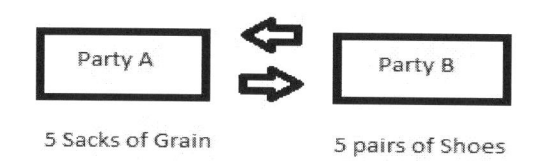

```
┌────────┐  ⇐   ┌────────┐
│ Party A │  ⇒   │ Party B │
└────────┘       └────────┘
5 Sacks of Grain    5 pairs of Shoes
```

The Natural Order of Goods exchange between two parties.

In Socialism, a totally different **Third Party** or **Party C** will intervene between **Parties A & B**, to control the natural exchange of goods and services.

Using the second illustration below, **Party C** will tell **Party A** to give him their five sacks of Grain and **Party B** give them the five pairs of Shoes. Once **Party C** has all the goods, **Party C** will attempt to negotiate with both **Parties A and B** and they [**Party C**] will be the deciding entity as to who gets what or how many each will get of the five sacks of grain or the five pairs of shoes, they now have.

```
          ┌─────────┐
          │ Party C │
          └─────────┘
               ⬇
┌─────────┐   ⬅   ┌─────────┐
│ Party A │       │ Party B │
└─────────┘   ➡   └─────────┘

5 sacks of Grain        5 Pairs of Shoes
```

```
          ┌─────────┐
          │ Party C │
          └─────────┘
             ⬆   ⬆
┌─────────┐       ┌─────────┐
│ Party A │       │ Party B │
└─────────┘       └─────────┘
```

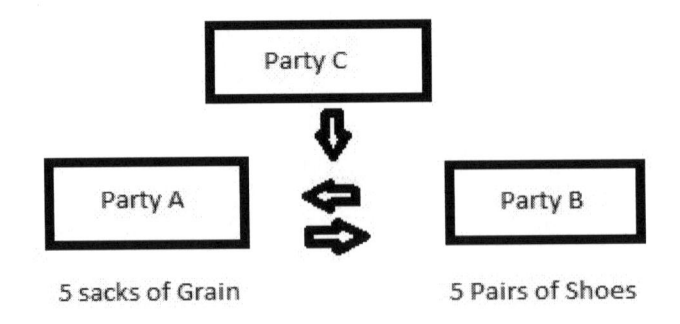

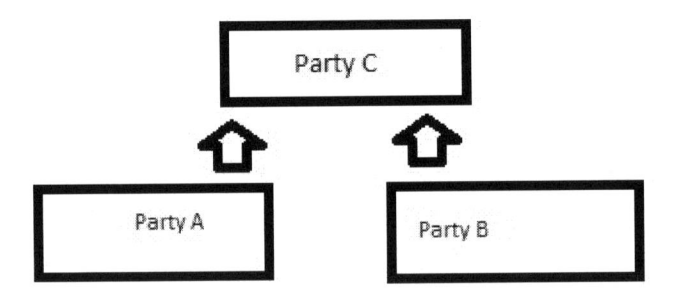

Both Parties A and B will give their goods to Party C

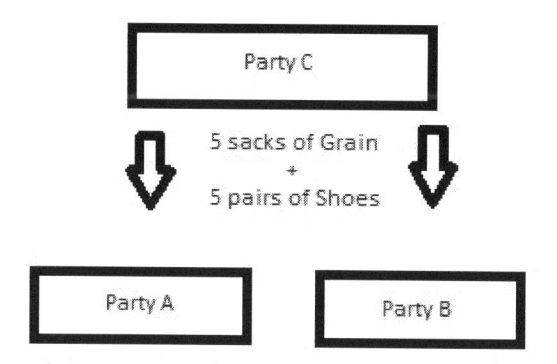

```
         ┌─────────────────┐
         │    Party C      │
         └─────────────────┘
              ⬇  5 sacks of Grain  ⬇
                       +
                 5 pairs of Shoes
  ┌──────────────┐          ┌──────────────┐
  │   Party A    │          │   Party B    │
  └──────────────┘          └──────────────┘
```

Party C determines the distribution of goods

However, Party C may make the decision to not give their goods to no one, including to both Parties A and B and decide to keep the sacks of grains and pairs of shoes to himself.

This is called "**Wealth Distribution**"!

This is also called "**Wealth Confiscation**"!

Furthermore, if Party C feels that Party A don't deserve five pairs of shoes, but only need two pairs of shoes instead, then Party C we only give that amount to Party A, whether the latter they like it or not. The same thing can go for Party B as well.

What just happened?

Party C received all the goods from both **Parties A & B**, and whatever decision Party C makes as to the distribution of these goods, both Parties A & B have-to accept the decision made, without any questions!

In other words, **Redistribution of Wealth** is in fact the stealing and theft of those who have something of value and is willingly given it to another outside entity, without recourse, who doesn't have or have not earned such gifts of value.

When Trade Unions were established in the United States over 130-plus years ago, their objective was to improve working conditions of the American Labor Force and protect the rights of workers from Employers who were abusing their work force.

For example, at California's **New Almaden Quicksilver Mines** during the 1870s and 1880s, Mine Workers were subjected to horrendous heat, flooding from monsoonal rains, poor shaft ventilation, while climbing handmade wood ladders when transiting in and out of the shafts. Understand, that this was during the time in American History, were electricity did not exist, Air Conditioning wasn't invented, and other technologies was non-existent, compared to mine conditions of today.

Workers of the New Almaden Quicksilver Mines were carrying Lead, Silver and Mercury ores in crudely-made sacks, which often weighed in excess of 200 pounds each. These sacks were carried by these mine workers with straps made up of hemp rope or burlap, secured to the tops of their heads for hours on end.

Many Mine Workers during the 19th and early 20th Century, died from disabilities, mine cave-ins, explosions, lung diseases, mine shaft fires, from suffocation due to the lack of oxygen and air inside these shafts.

It was during this time Labor Unions were solely needed to hold Employers like the New Almaden Quicksilver Mines Company accountable for their actions and worked with them to improve the Employee's work conditions. Back then, they were instrumental in forcing Employers into creating better work environments, better pay, increase promotion opportunities and minimizing hazards in the workplace.[40]

That was then and this is now.

Today, Labor Unions are no longer interested in the act to compromise between Employers and Employees.

In 21st Century America, Labor Unions now make huge profits off the back off both the Workers and the Employers. They do this via Collective Bargaining Agreements, Employee Union Dues and manipulating the workforce via Ideological Subversion, that they, the Unions, are fighting for "**Workers Rights**" or "**Working Class Americans**".

<u>In-reality they are not.</u>

Picture of the Madison, Wisconsin Union Protests against Wisconsin's Union Busting Bill in 2010.

(Courtesy of Colorful Revolution)

Labor Unions of today, are conducting extortion operations and tactics, similar-to the Italian Mafia, to make huge sums of money, adding up to billions of dollars in revenue.

That's not all.

Big Labor Unions now control the American Workforce, using the threats of strikes, violence and open protests, to the point where their actions not only become a hinderance to the Employer, but to the Employee, to include that industry's economy as well.

One must ask themselves, who benefits from these strikes or Collective Bargaining Agreements, negotiations and activities?

The answer; the Union Bosses and their leaders!

It's a message aimed at the "evil and wealthy" CEOs and "Capitalists" throughout the nation, that they, the Public Service Unions, have the upper hand and the absolute power that controls the workforce in America, not them.

This is the reason why you have violence, paid demonstrations, family intimidation, horrendous negative media coverage, during strikes aimed at these Employers. Because Marxists, who are operating the Unions, has taken away the natural ability for human-to-human relations, by placing such ability into the hands of a third party.

And another aspect when Demoralizing the nation when it comes to Labor Relations, the union bosses who are high ranking members of Communist Organizations, such as CPUSA and Democratic Socialists of America (DSA), often hide their true intentions other than made up mantra labeled as "workers' rights".

There are no workers' rights when it comes to public service unions!

You either submit to them are you will pay the price!

The one-time tradition of an Employee selling and profiting off his or her skills, needed to produce goods and services, have now been hijacked by the unions via Marxist propaganda rhetoric pushing the **"Workers' Rights"** lie.

In 21st century America, Big Labor Unions has gotten to the point, where unions members are unelected, Ideological bureaucrats, who have now obtained unchecked, unlimited power of the Employee to control the ladder's actions as they see fit.

Labor Union organizations also have their own Public Relations (PR) Departments, that uses the unelected media to force their Employees to push the Employer for more pay and more benefits than they already have.

A great example of the ladder is the push by the Unions, the propagandized media and the American Communist Party. for the increase of **Minimum Wage pay to $15 dollars per hour**, for workers who have little or no skills to perform their jobs.[41,42]

This lie, have already been enacted by several states, such as Washington, Oregon, California and Illinois, using the made-up mantra of Employers not paying a so-called **"Living Wage"** to unskilled laborers.

<u>The fake narrative in which Marxist Propagandists in power is to advocate the raising of the Minimum Wage to now (key word is now) $15 per hour, so that low-income Employees can feed a family of four.</u>

Of course, this is not the reason why the Minimum Wage was set into law. It was not intended to feed a family of four, but was supposed to give the opportunity of Entry-Level, low-skilled, or non-skilled laborers the chance to work, as a start, to further receive training and education, so they can become skilled laborers, with added pay and benefits for them to increase their standards of life in the long-term.

Photos of protestors advocating to increase the National Minimum Wage Rate from $7.25 to $15.00 per hour.

(Courtesy of Slate.com and Chicago Tribune)

However, Marxists in Big Labor Unions and their Liberal Dupes know this to be fact, yet they are advocating the raising of the Minimum Wage. **The reasoning behind such effort; to make it appear that the Unions are trying to Redistribute the Wealth of Employers to the Employees.**

Remember the old saying; "perception is only 9/10ths of reality".

Understand, the ones who are going to get hurt by raising the Minimum Wage are the ***Employees, not the Employers***.

Minimum Wage Laws are set in the United States based on the Federal Labor Laws, which requires Employers to pay their workers the minimum wage amount, which is, as of this writing, $7.25 per hour.

Labor laws are managed by the Department of Labor (DOL). The intent for paying Minimum Wage, is to set the minimum amount of money an Employer should pay their workers to perform jobs or tasks which requires little or no education, or no skill set to conduct as previously mentioned.

Minimum wage pay is only *temporary* for the low-skilled worker. If the Employee want to make more than Minimum Wage, to improve their quality of life, Employers are required, by law, to offer their Employees the incentive to apply for better pay skilled-jobs, via On-the-Job Training (OJT) or other education incentive, such as earning a technical or vocational certificate or college degree.

This opportunity also extends to persons in the United States regardless of Race or Gender in accordance with Title 7, of the Civil Rights Act of 1964.[43,44]

To be fair, the following paragraph is about Minimum Wage in America and is based-on fact, via the Department of Labor (DOL), in which Marxist Men and their Liberal Dupes, refuse to tell you, as they spread their lies and distortion of fact in the media.

What laws governs the nation's Minimum Wage?

The **Fair Labor Standards Act of 1938 (Amended May 2011) and 29 Code of Federal Regulations (CFR), Chapter V-Wage and Hour Division, Department of Labor.**[45,46,47]

In-reality, of the 50 states and 5 US territories within the Union of the United States, Federal Labor Laws have given the States flexibility, for Employers to pay either more or less than the set $7.25 per hour wage based upon many factors. One such factor that is calculated in the Minimum Wage standard is the **Consumer Price Index (CPI)**.[48]

Of the 50 states, 5 U.S. Territories and the District of Columbia (as of January 1, 2019);

29 States in 3 territories and the District of Columbia pay greater than the federal minimum wage of $7.25 per hour.

17 States and one Territory, Puerto Rico, pay the federal minimum wage

5 States pay no minimum wage however Federal Law does apply.

One territory, the Commonwealth of the Northern Mariana Islands (CNMI), pays less than minimum wage which is $7.05 per hour

One territory, American Samoa, pays minimum wage as set by that particular-industry, ranging from $4.98 per hour and $6.39 per an hour.

Marxists propagandists will push their lies and deception on the American public regarding Minimum Wage via Communist Front Groups such as;

> **Black Lives Matter**
>
> **#Me TOO! Movement**
>
> **LBGTQ Movement**
>
> **Democratic Socialists of America (DSA)**
>
> **Young Socialist League (YSL)**
>
> **And many others**

Front Groups such as the after-mentioned, would take to the streets using organized and paid protesters, alongside with Big Labor Union members and protest outside of businesses targeted by Marxists Propagandists, to force businesses into paying the $15 per hour Minimum Wage. All of these made up protests, stirred on by the unelected media, to present such protest as legitimate, will chat "Workers' Rights" and label such CEOs and Business Owners as "evil and greedy".

Study after exhaustive study, numerous Federal Government agencies, the Department of Labor (DOL), the Bureau of Economic Analysis (BEA) and private groups, such as the Tax Foundation, and the Heritage Foundation, have demonstrated that by raising the Minimum Wage will **increase unemployment** of Low-Skilled workers and **increase the price of goods and services**.

In 2019, the same Low-Skilled Workers in which Big Labor Unions and Marxist Organizations such as the American Communist Party, have destroyed Low-Skilled Worker's positions, as Employers are replacing their positions with computer automation.

Yet the Marxists at CPUSA and Big Labor Union bosses, like the AFL-CIO, will constantly tell you, that they are for the "Rights of the Workers", when they are only out for themselves!

This "Raising the Minimum Wage" to 15 per hour, is utter nonsense, it is needed to be exposed for what it is.

An absolute lie!

Equality

This word has now become the American Left's favorite cliché next to "Workers' Rights", "Women's Reproductive Rights", "Environmental Justice", "Earth Justice" "Social Justice" and "Civil Rights".

That word is **Equality**.

The actual definition of Equality is the quality or state of being equal are on-par with your fellow peer group.[49]

Since Marxist Propagandas always tell the public, that we are all equal-to-one-another, the question should be asked; ***are we all equal-to-each-other?***

On outside of our biological existence, Man or Woman (nothing in between) or Cultural make up, meaning Black, White and indifferent, are we truly equal?

Even in the Holy Bible, Equality is **not mentioned** anywhere inside its pages. Now, it does say that we are all the children of God, and each one of us is created in the image of him, but it does not say that we are equal-to-each-other?

So, are we?

The answer is no!

In the Judeo-Christian Religion, what we learned during our time on Earth and what we do in life, determines who we are. Our actions in life determines whether-or-not you would enter the Kingdom of God (Heaven) come Judgment Day or be sent to the Dungeons of Hell, where Satan and his Angel Lucy await you in the Lake of Fire.

Yet, Marxists want you to believe, that if we destroy Capitalism/Americanism, along with the principles of Free-Market Competition, and usher in Socialism, everything and everyone will be equal-to-each-other.

It is a flat out lie!

We are not equal-to-each-other!

Just imagine, that some of us are taller, shorter in height with each other, some people have different and economic backgrounds, different upbringings, different cultures, different genders, and the list goes on.

However, Marxism teaches, that for one to have Universal Peace and Universal Prosperity, you must be forced (leap) to accept the concept of equality within a society, which includes all this basic in social political structures!

$$\neq$$

Marxist Propagandists, in the Demoralization phase of Ideological Subversion, will continue to hammer such lies and deception to both the younger generation and the older ones, took convince such people that Equality is possible once Socialism is implemented first, then Full-Communism last.

The keyword; **Equality is possible**. No

Not one Marxist has ever admitted, that Equality can be successfully done, in real-life and in real society!

Just think of all what happened, if you build a house of Equality on a ground of quicksand. Sooner or later, the house wouldn't not only collapse under its own weight, but will be consumed and buried in ground, in which its foundation once sat.

This is exactly what happens, when Socialism is implemented anywhere is been tried. It will collapse on his own, because of the inefficiency it creates, by destroying any and all incentives for man to produce.

Also, Socialism/Communism forces people against their will to live, work and survive in economic environment, where they work for free to support those who have no incentive to produce!

This last fact is _exactly_ will both Karl Marx in Friedrich Engels missed come on when they wrote the **Communist Manifesto** and their failed attempt to understand Capitalism/Free-Market Principles! The latter economic system has been proven over-and-over again, throughout Human history, to increase the standard living throughout the world, because individual ideas, innovation to create better products and services and to incentivize Man in-order for Nations and whole societies to flourish!

Socialism has done the very opposite!

So, in the sense of Equality, as yourself the following questions;

Are we Equal in obtaining the same opportunities to be successful, by going to school at night, working to get that college degree, to obtain better employment, or working during the weekends, than the people who do not have the initiative to do the same thing to improve their standards of living?

Are we Equal among each other, when some of us work one or two jobs at a time, being away from our love ones for hours on end, and some instances months on end, to provide food on the table, roof over our heads, while some people within the population, we have no initiative to hold a job at all?

Are we Equal to the Illegal Alien Immigrant, who sneaks into our country via the Southern Border with Mexico, coming from Socialist-ravaged places, and come into our American cities, and become lazy bastards by not seeking employment, bad mouthing our country, while simultaneously sponging off the money, paid by the American Taxpayers in the form Government Entitlements?

Are we Equal to each other, when the same Illegal Alien who doesn't work, or pay taxes, but qualifies in so-called "Sanctuary Cities and States", to receive Unemployment Insurance, Health Care and Treatment, Food Stamps, and Disability Pay, clogging up the Welfare system, where real Americans who are in need of such assistance standby and wait for years, to receive such assistance, as their disability worsens?

Are we Equal to the so-called "Loving Criminal" Drug Abuser, Drug Dealers, Violent Gang Member, who are known criminals, who floods our border, from places like El Salvador, Honduras, Iran, Afghanistan, Syria, Libya, Palestine, Somalia and Yemen, to bad mouth our country and cause harm to American citizens on our own soil?

Are we Equal to the so-called "Loving Criminal" who, not only abuses narcotics, cocaine, or methamphetamines, but while influenced on these substances, conducts crimes from Petty Larceny to First-Degree Murder, while the rest of us law-abiding citizens who does not break any laws or use illicit drugs whatsoever?

Ask yourself these questions.

Yet still, Marxist Propagandists continue to push the lie of Equality down the throats of that American people.

Why?

Because such propagandists have been brainwashed to accept, the blatant lies and distortion of reality, thinking that Equality is something everybody wants!

And will try their damnedest to convince you to think otherwise.

No, people do not want Equality, people desire Freedom!

Remember, Marxists have been trained to push the American people in the direction that they want you to go in, which is why they harped on the lie of Equality, Equality, Equality.

People desire the **Freedom** to choose to do, what they want to do, by learning as much as we can, work hard and receive recognition or monetary awards for our earned abilities.

The people want a safe environment, so that our God-given Right to own property, protect our family and ourselves, against those who attempt to transgress against us, so we all can strive to have better future, for ourselves and even for our descendants who haven't been born yet.

People desire **Freedom** to become successful, because we are not equal-to-each-other! We are all from different cultures, different backgrounds, and harbor different ideas to spearhead innovation to make life easier in the future.

People desire the **Freedom** to have constant competition, constant perfection, which our Forefathers envisioned, where we can help each other, build each other up, because we are so different from each other!

Equality is a farce!

And there are many Marxists who know this!

Chapter Five: Destabilization

"America is like a healthy body and its resistance is threefold; its Patriotism, its Morality and its Spiritual life. If we can undermine these three areas, America will collapse from within."

~Joseph Stalin~[1]

The second phase during Ideological Subversion is the process called **Destabilization**.

During Destabilization, the goal of the Marxists on all levels of American Society is this; to destroy the United States of America from within.

To do this, they have-to create the conditions to completely render the Geo-political environment of the United States ineffective to protect itself, to the point where the entire country will end up in a Civil War.

Yuri Bezmenov describe this phenomenon, where Marxists and their propaganda machine, will begin to radicalize three main areas of the country, which provides societal stabilization-as-a-whole.[2]

They are;

> *The Economy*
>
> *Law and Order/Military*
>
> *Media (even more)*

The Economy

When it comes to the destabilization of the American economy, the first thing the Marxists and their Useful Liberal Dupes will try to do, is destabilized all attempts and all actions dealing with the Bargaining process of Labor Relations.

Labor Relations between Big Corporations and Small Businesses will have within its confines, militant Communist Front Group members like the **LBGTQ** movement when it comes to gender, the **Council Against Religious Discrimination (CARD)** when it comes to religion, the **Council on American-Islamic Relations (CAIR)** when it comes to Muslim relations, and the **NAACP** when it comes to Black Americans and **La Raza (the Race)** when it comes to Hispanic American relations. These businesses are all operated funded and trained by Marxists leading these groups, who in-turn, take their orders directly from the **American Communist Party (CPUSA)**.

This inclusive of list of groups will fundamentally destroy any it all Employer-Employee relations, using the banners of **"Gender Equality"** or **"Gender Discrimination"**, **"Religious Equality"** or **"Religious Discrimination"**, **"Islamophobia"**, and **"Civil Rights"**.

Other influential organizations such as the **American Federation of Labor and Congress of Industrial Relations (AFL-CIO)** would wield enormous lobbying power to get their way in the halls of Congress.[3,4,5]

The AFL-CIO fully controls every aspect of over 69-plus Public Union affiliates and their influence, money from the Communist donors and Union Dues, are all contributing to the Destabilization process of the United States.

The AFL-CIO is by far the largest Communist Front Group outside of the American Communist Party, which is the leading charged for U.S. Employers to give low-skilled and non-skilled laborers $15 per hour Minimum Wage! This group led by **Richard Trumpka**, is also behind the lobbying effort to destroy the "**Right-to-Work Legislation**" which prohibit union security agreements between Employers and Public Unions.

The after-mentioned legislation which are being passed by state legislatures, also prevent Employees who work in the Public Service Industry (Hospitals, Grocery Stores, etc.) from being forced into joining their respective industry's Union, thus decreasing the Union Dues being embezzled from the Workers by Union Bosses to fund their lobbying efforts in Congress.

For clarity, the AFL-CIO is against **any legislation** that prevents them the total power to hustle, extort, harass, and even control every aspect of unionized labor.

As of this writing 2019 come there are 29 states that has Right-to-Work Laws on the books and is gaining momentum in many other states as well.[6,7]

During Destabilization, Labor Activists become violent to those employers who "outright reject their demands". Some actions included vandalism, property damage is to businesses, blackmailing corporation Board of Directors, CEOs and Upper/Middle Management. Other tactics which Labor Activists have employed were, imitation threats, false media attention and even laying charges of Sexual Harassment or Assault on corporation members, without providing any proof to back up such allegations.

For example, in March 2011, 15 Republican State Senators in Wisconsin, receive the following death threat email from a Marshalls, Wisconsin Union activist;[8]

From: XXXX
Sent: Wed 3/9/2011 9:18 PM
To: Sen.Kapanke; Sen.Darling; Sen.Cowles; Sen.Ellis; Sen.Fitzgerald; Sen.Galloway; Sen.Grothman; Sen.Harsdorf; Sen.Hopper; Sen.Kedzie; Sen.Lasee; Sen.Lazich; Sen.Leibham; Sen.Moulton; Sen.Olsen
Subject: Atten: Death threat!!!! Bomb!!!!

Please put your things in order because you will be killed and your familes will also be killed due to your actions in the last 8 weeks. Please explain to them that this is because if we get rid of you and your families then it will save the rights of 300,000 people and also be able to close the deficit that you have created. I hope you have a good time in hell. Read below for more information on possible scenarios in which you will die.

WE want to make this perfectly clear. Because of your actions today and in the past couple of weeks I and the group of people that are working with me have decided that we've had enough. We feel that you and the people that support the dictator have to die. We have tried many other ways of dealing with your corruption but you have taken things too far and we will not stand for it any longer. So, this is how it's going to happen: I as well as many others know where you and your family live, it's a matter of public records.

We have all planned to assult you by arriving at your house and putting a nice little bullet in your head. However, we decided that we wouldn't leave it there. We also have decided that this may not be enough to send the message to you since you are so "high" on Koch and have decided that you are now going to single handedly make this a dictatorship instead of a democrasic process. So we have also built several bombs that we have placed in various locations around the areas in which we know that you frequent.

This includes, your house, your car, the state capitol, and well I won't tell you all of them because that's just no fun. Since we know that you are not smart enough to figure out why this is happening to you we have decided to make it perfectly clear to you. If you and your goonies feel that it's necessary to strip the rights of 300,000 people and ruin their lives, making them unable to feed, clothe, and provide the necessities to their families and themselves then We Will "get rid of" (in which I mean kill) you. Please understand that this does not include the heroic Rep. Senator that risked everything to go aganist what you and your goonies wanted him to do. We feel that it's worth our lives to do this, because we would be saving the lives of 300,000 people. Please make your peace with God as soon as possible and say goodbye to your loved ones we will not wait any longer. YOU WILL DIE!!!!

(Courtesy Patterio.com)

In the Destabilization process, the inability to compromise even reaches whole families, neighbors and between Educators versus Students or Educator versus Parents.[9]

Neighbors cannot compromise with each other, to resolve problems between themselves, which will benefit both parties. Neighbors even went as far as to seek revenge upon each other, where violent confrontations would erupt, causing severe property damage, criminal intimidation and even murder. Oftentimes, neighbors will take each other to Civil Court to resolve their disputes, instead of sitting down and talking with each other to find a sensible solution to the dispute.

Inside the home there is no difference.

Whole families no longer compromise between themselves. Understanding, this is always been the case in the past and some family members for often shunned by other relatives, because of their personal interaction with the so-called "Wrong People".

However, during the Destabilization process in America, husband and wife no longer can compromise with each other, no matter whether the issue is trivial in nature, or large. Parents and Kids become increasingly more confrontational, to the point where verbal and/or physical confrontations occur, which often split the family apart.

In very few cases, even though it does happen, families have resorted to physical violence between each other, using weapons, poisons, intimidation and revenge against each other, to the point where lives are ruin, bodily harm is ensued or incident which could lead to deaths/murder have occurred.

One must remember, that in-order for Socialism to take place, the social unit such as the Family, must be destroyed in its entirety. And during the Destabilization, in a country like the United States, the destruction of the family is seen as more prevalent than ever before as in anytime in American History.

Relation between Teachers and Students no longer exist. It must be repeated that Teachers are viewed by the younger generation as authority figures, thus in Ideological Subversion, Teacher are no longer respected by the ladder. Children who are of Elementary, Junior High and High School age, become confrontational either verbally or physically with Educators, School Administrators, and Principals of schools.

Such actions by these students, they will be sent to **Juvenile Detention (JDC)** or other **Special Education and Needs Programs** now in place in schools, to deal with the "emotional problems" of the after-mentioned students. Once they are in the system of the Juvenile Courts, such kids become labeled as "Troublemakers" or "Deviant Criminals" who are "Uncontrollable" and will never have a chance to lead a good life.

Relationships between Teachers and Parents are also destabilized, to the point where the parents will blame the child's behavior on the Teacher and School District, instead of the accepting responsibility for themselves.

Understand, learning starts in the home, and once the home and the family has been destroyed beyond repair, learning and discipline is destroyed beyond repair as well. This is exactly what Marxists want done in America.

As previously mentioned in the last chapter during the Demoralization of the United States of America, riots and picketers during strikes, and criminals are hailed as heroes by the Unelected Marxist propagandized media. Their blatant actions of insurrection of violence, looting, burning of private property, along with confrontations with Law Enforcement, is portrayed as "a normal way of life in America", for which it is not!

An example of the latter, can be illustrated when Marxists in positions of power and prestige, exacerbated the shooting deaths of known criminals and their confrontational actions with those in positions of authority, such as **Treyvon Martin** in Sanford Florida, **Michael Brown** in Ferguson Missouri, **Freddie Gray** in Baltimore Maryland, and other incidents, involving Black Men and the Police.

You would know when Marxists is attempting to Destabilize the country, when some people in American Society, often feel like they are **"walking on egg shells"**, or **"everybody has a chip on their shoulder"**.

Sometimes people have the fear of retaliation from those who they perceive words or phrases might offend the other person.

The late Author, Journalist, Assistant Secretary of State under President John F. Kennedy and US Ambassador to Finland under President Lyndon B. Johnson, **Carl T. Rowan (1925-2000)** sums up the destabilization process in human relations;[11]

"There are two ways to circumvent, or trampled over a Constitution, however ingenuously contrived maybe it's Democratic precepts. One way is to arouse public fear and hatred to a point where all concepts of minority protection, or right of dissent, gets swept away in a tide of emotion…The second way is to abrogate a Constitution is to a mass enough police or military power to force your will upon society".

There is a plethora of examples which can be found, proving Ambassador Rowan's statement above. Here are some examples;

Fort Hood Massacre-2009

Little Rock Arkansas Attack-2009

Sandy Hook Elementary School Shooting-2012

Boston Marathon Terror Attack-2013

Moore Oklahoma Beheading-2014

Chattanooga, Tennessee Terror Attack-2015

San Bernardino, California Massacre-2015

New York City/New Jersey Bombing-2016

St. Cloud, Minnesota Hatchet Attack-2016

Pulse Nightclub Massacre-2016

A better example can be illustrated when one look at the main element of the Republican Party of the United States. Since its creation in Wisconsin 1854, the Republican Party have been the outspoken voice of action, legislation of Equal Rights guaranteed under the US Constitution, and now fighting to block the Communist-Left's plan to instill Socialism in America.

As a response to the Conservative-Republican Wing of the party, the Unelected Marxist Media, has put up wave after wave of lies, disinformation, and character assassination of those aligns themselves with or support the actions of the Republican Party.

For those who have been subverted into believing that Marxism will make a better world for everybody around the world, falsely of course, violent actions perpetrated by the media, have called some too emotionally take such confrontations into their own hands, to silent any and all opposition to the Communist Order.

Photo of Assassin James Hodgkinson, 66 of Bellville Illinois.

On June 14th, 2017 in Alexandria Virginia, a suburb of Washington DC, the United States Congress was prepared to play their annual congressional baseball game for charity. The game, scheduled for the next day, pitted the Democrat Party versus the Republican Party in the game which would have drawn both political parties in unison for one day, away from politics.[12,13,14,15]

That day no one expect, that the practice game was going to turn into small massacre.

James Hodgkinson, 66 of Belleville Illinois, located outside of Saint Louis Missouri, was an active supporter of Marxist Senator from Vermont Bernie Sanders, traveled to the Washington D.C. area and to take the so-called "Communist Revolution" into his own hands.

Erivan at the Alexandria Virginia park on with an SKS rifle, and two semi-automatic Smith and Weston pistols, open fire in broad daylight at the 15 to 20 members of the Republican Party Congressmen practicing.

Soon a 10-minute fire fight ensued between Hodgkinson, Capitol Police, Alexandria City Police and the U.S. Secret Service details who were there to protect the Congressmen.

During the violent confrontation, Louisiana Republican Congressman and House of Representative Minority Whip Steven Scalise with savagely wounded, along with Tyson Foods lobbyist Matt Mika, Capitol Police Officers David Bailey and Crystal Griner and Jack Barth. The latter was an aide to Texas Republican Congressman Roger Williams.

Hodgkinson was killed during the incident.

After this tragic incident, James Hodgkinson wasn't the only one who have called for the murdering of Conservative-Republicans, because latter is fighting Marxists in this country who want to fundamentally transform the United States into a Soviet Union-type Russia.

Duped Useful Idiot Liberals, who have been subverted by the Marxist Elites, have not only taken to Social Media platforms, but some have come out openly on Television and in public, advocating the inhumane killing Conservative voices!

An example of this can be seen on the Social Media giant Twitter, after the wounding a Congressman Steve Scalise, by unknown persons who have spewed hatred for Scalise and praised Hodgkinson for the latter's actions;[16,17]

"If the KKK support Steve Scalise dies, the shooter deserves a holiday, true leadership. Now the Trumps, Kush and Miller need to be transitioned."

Or;

"If the shooter [Hodgkinson] has a serious health condition then taking potshots at the GOP [Grand Old Party] leadership considered self-defense?"

Sometimes, such threats are often lobbied by the Marxist-Leninists in positions of power such as Democrat Congressman Paul Kanjorski of Pennsylvania;

> *"That Scott [Rick Scott, now a U.S. Senator] down there running for Governor of Florida. Instead of running for Governor of Florida they ought to have him and shoot him. Put him up against the wall and shoot him. He stole billions of dollars from the United States Government and he's running for Governor of Florida. He's a Millionaire and a Billionaire. He is no hero he's a damn crook. Is just we don't prosecute big crooks."*

Remember, this is coming from Congressman Kanjorski who serves as a U.S. Congressman, talking and making threats like this!

Then again, Congressman Kanjorski need to speak for himself when it comes to **"prosecuting big crooks"**. **The entire American Communist establishment should be prosecuted to the full extent of the law for being the crooks and the mobs which they are!**

Yet, they are not.

Law and Order

During the second stage of Ideological Subversion, Law and Order is becoming more ineffective than they have been during the Demoralization stage.

Here the Courts, which are now occupied by Radical Leftist Judges, Lawyers and Aides, who have been trained and both Law School by Radical Professors, prevent legal challenges in selective Court cases, which are deemed to go against the Communist Order.

Any Judicial case, which favors Americanism, the rule of law based on the precepts of the U.S. Constitution will automatically be ruled as "illegitimate". In other words, any legal case that is considered moral, just and good, which protects the people of the United States, are to be ruled by these handpicked Radical Judges as being "immoral", "un-equal and infringes on the Civil Rights of people", when reality such cases are not.

Marxist and subverted Dupes in both the United States Congress and in State Legislatures, will begin to give the Judicial system of the United States of America, the power to both Legislate Laws and enforce such laws from the bench!

<u>**The empowerment of the courts to legislate from the bench has for decades, permeated the Supreme Court a United States (SCOTUS), Federal District Courts, Military Courts, Criminal and Civil Courts which includes law enforcement giants, such as the Department of Justice (DOJ) and the Federal Bureau of Investigations (FBI).**</u>

By weakening law and order within the country, Marxists have a goal to create a **Two-Tier Justice System**, within the Judicial Branch of Government; <u>**one for the opposition**</u> and <u>**one for themselves**</u>.

Just a *thought* of having a Two-Tier Justice System in America should frighten us all!

One must remember, that in W. Cleon Skosen's book ***The Naked Communist***, where he lists the 45 Communist Goals, where Marxist-Leninists plan to take over the United States of America via a Civil War. One way for "a glorious Communist Revolution" to take place on American soil, is to have a number-of ideological-trained Marxists, operating in key positions within the Department of Justice **to gain control and dismantle the FBI**.[18]

Radical members with in the Justice Department hierarchy, will seek to **"stack the courts"** with like-minded Marxists to serve as members of Grand Juries, Federal Court-appointed and unaccountable Judges like the **Foreign Intelligence Surveillance Act Court (FISA)** or put their own selected number of "Judicial Activists" Judges in all 11 District Courts throughout America.[19, 20, 21]

The Communist and Socialist Parties of the United States will also allow their influence to further contaminate the U.S. Judicial System, by placing Marxists to run for elections to serve as Federal Prosecutors as well.

These courts, along with the Communist Justices and Grand Juries, will be used to conduct "**political witch hunts**" or <u>**made-up fabricated allegations and investigations to destroy any and all opposition to the Communist Order.**</u> Such political witch hunts, that are played out in the unelected Marxist Media as being real, are not grounded in any reality or any real evidence at all.

The idea behind these blatant unconstitutional and needless investigations, all paid for by American Taxpayer money, is to send a message to those who has future-plans to go against the Marxists in positions of Power and Prestige; **for them not to challenge them, unless they will accuse you of something in order to destroy you.**

Secondly, Communists will use the stacking of the courts to further destabilize the country's Judicial System, while simultaneously tearing down the American Judicial System in total.[21,22,23,24]

The best example of this, can be illustrated in the baseless, fact-less and political witch hunt, involving the unaccountable, taxpayer-funded Robert J. Mueller Special Counsel investigation into the so-called "**Russian Collusion**" between Russian President Vladimir Putin and then-Presidential Candidate Donald J. Trump.[25,26,27,28]

Other examples include;

The Repeal of the Defense of Marriage Act of 1996 (DOMA)[29]

Roe vs. Wade Supreme Court Decision on Abortion[30]

The push by Congress to repeal the U.S. Constitution's Second Amendment

The push to bankrupt the Oil, Natural Gas and Coal industries and replace them with "Green Energy"

Another excellent example, where the American judicial system of law and order based on the U.S. Constitution, is the fact that our founding document has been and current is being discredited overseas. Many of the disinformation campaigns and lies were done by numerous Marxist Politicians over the recent years and even conducted by a sitting Supreme Court Justice; **Ruth Bader Ginsburg**.

Hailed as a heroine by the Communist Left for her radical court decisions, which had gone against the U.S. Constitution, a document which he was sworn to uphold, Justice Ginsburg (A.K.A. "**The Notorious RBG**" coined by Communist Black Hollywood, half-baked and Useful Idiot Comedian **D. L. Hughley**), went to Egypt and discredited American Judicial System and the American Constitutional process.

Of course, this incident has long been forgotten with-the-exception being refreshed in the reader's mind right here in this book.

Supreme Court Justice Ruth Bader Ginsburg, The Notorious R.B.G., was interviewed in February 2012 by Al Hayat Television in Cairo Egypt. When she visited there, she met so-called "fellow Revolutionaries" or members of the ultra-left Radical group the Muslim Brotherhood and had this to say regarding new countries being created around the world in forming their own government;[31]

"I would not look to the U.S. Constitution if I were drafting a constitution in year 2012. I might look at the Constitution of South Africa. That was a deliberate attempt to have a fundamental instrument of government the embrace human rights, have an independent Judiciary. It really is, I think, a great piece of work that was done."

No Justice R.B.G.!

The South African Constitution and its Judiciary System was not a great piece of work!

The constitution in South Africa, was made by Marxists like yourself, where the Judges inside their Judicial system are the Accuser, the Jury, the Judge and the Executioner, all being done inside "Kangaroo"-type court trials! The procedure is done inside of South African Courts, are same way which was done inside the U.S. Senate in November 2018, during the confirmation hearings against former Washington D.C. Federal Judge Brett Kavanaugh's appointment to the Supreme Court.

Those who are accused of crimes, whether real or made-up, in South Africa, are tried and convicted in court without Due Process or to have the opportunity to obtain legal representation.

Yet, there is a sitting Supreme Court Justice, who is being interviewed in a foreign land, speaking with a news organization, which has known ties to Muslim Extremism, as outlined by U.S. Intelligence agencies, as their mouthpiece to push propaganda, **<u>by discrediting her own country's constitution which she has sworn to uphold and defend for decades!</u>**

One-last avenue, where Marxists take when traveling down the road to destabilize the country's law and order, is their constant attempts to render law enforcement agencies around the nation and on every level ineffective.

Because of the unelected media hype, lies and disinformation campaigns, especially during the Barack Obama's Administration, which was occupied by numerous self-proclaimed Communists and Socialists, in the wake of the White-on-Black Police shootings, such as **Trayvon Martin**, and **Michael Brown**, the Department of Justice has implemented strict policing polices to law enforcement agencies, to render them ineffective.

Now called "**Community Policing**", hundreds of Law Enforcement Agencies have been trained to be "**sensitive to communities**", especially Minority Communities, or "Persons of Color", to <u>**understand**</u> the criminal's plight as to why they commit the acts of violence, family abuse and use drugs and live the way they live.

It's a bunch of nonsense!

Cities across the American landscape, such as Chicago Illinois Ferguson Missouri, St. Louis, Missouri, Baltimore Maryland, New York City, and many others have had Marxist Mayors, Religious "Social Justice Warrior" Clergy, Federal and State Politicians, have met together to pass legislation and create city ordinances, to render such law enforcement agencies useless to defend the law-abiding public.

To their credit, Marxists have done a wonderful job in this area of Destabilizing Law and Order, because their never ending lies, deception and attacks on Law Enforcement, using Hollywood, the Unelected Media and Social Media platforms to instilled in the mines of the young, that Cops and Police are corrupt, they are racists, bigoted and they have a self-superiority complex, when it comes to Minority groups.

Everything is built on a bunch of lies.

Of course, Communist Propagandists will subvert the heads of the latter population, that there is a plethora of "**Systematic Racism**" when it comes to law enforcement personnel and lie constantly that "**police**

brutality" against "persons of color" happens all the time, despite of the lack of evidence supporting such claim.[32]

Law enforcement agencies now have-to be extra careful in performing their dangerous job to protect the public and need to be more aware of their surroundings, while on the job. Police Officers have-to even more attuned in their jobs, as to how they deal with Criminals.

Why?

Because, Police have-to do this out the fear of retaliation, by groups like **Black Lives Matter (BLM)**, which is led by the **lily-white Communist Shaun King**, who have himself called for "**open season**" to murder in cold-blood Cops doing their duties to protect the public.[33]

Other groups, such as La Raza, Black Anarchical Groups, such as the **Nation of Islam (NOI)**, **New Black Panther Party (NBPP)** and **Black Israelites**, will become confrontational with the Police, with the purpose of destroying them because they have believed in the lies which Communists have advertised every day. These after-mentioned groups have been subverted to have no respect for the law or law enforcement or for those who support law enforcement.

Lastly the Marxists in position of power and prestige, when it comes to the Destabilization of Law and Order of United States is done by the flood of Illegal Immigration into our country.

This topic would be further discussed it in next chapter, called **Crisis,** but nevertheless, Communists in Congress and in the media, to include those who are on every level of society, is calling for **Open Borders** and abolishing the **Immigration, Customs and Enforcement (ICE)** agency for disrupting illegal and unvetted foreigners from entering the United States.[34,35]

Both CPUSA and SPUSA (the American Communist and Socialist Parties) have tried and will continue to try to legislate, mobilize thousands and conduct their never-ending propaganda campaigns to abolish ICE and abolish Law Enforcement as well. They truly believe, what Karl Marx has written in the ***Communist Manifesto***, that Law and Order was put into place by the Bourgeoisie to keep the Proletariat from obtaining the former's riches.

Such adherence these lies and deceptions of reality, is dangerous and it is up to the reader to comprehend and understand that such evil people in positions of power, are really trying to destroy Law and Order in our country.

This can not be disputed!

The Media

<u>In the Destabilization process, the American Media no longer reports the news, but have filled their ranks with radicalized Ideological subverted activists, who dress themselves up as Journalists.</u>

Since the 1980s, the media has placed itself to go against societal norms and have become the Communist propaganda machine of the Marxist Left.

Their job in the 21st century, is the further alienate the population of the United States, by creating "fake news stories" and artificially made-up, manufactured crisis, to control public emotions, steer public opinion in the way they want to and keep the rest of the public agitated.[36,37,38]

In other words, force your Socialist Agenda down the throats of the American people, whether they like it or not.

As previously mentioned, such news organizations like the Cable News Network (CNN), MSNBC, ABC, CBS, NPR, PBS, and others, collude with each other to formulate "narratives" or stories, in-order to spread their lies, disinformation campaigns, and to measure their subversive tactics, to see whether they are effective or not.

The reason why these media organizations continue to do such evil deeds, is to keep the American people agitated, filled with rage, hate and discontent, to such an extent, that their reporting of "fake news" will further divide this country, to destabilize our sacred institutions and bring it to Crisis.[37,38]

Yes, even the half-baked, uneducated so-called Journalists in the media will advocate for violence and the silencing of any and all opposition of those who refuse to accept the Communist Order. These mentally inept Journalists, will tote the Communist line, using the clichés of "Social Justice", "Equality", "Fairness" or "Civil Rights".

The new American Media is also influenced by outside Marxists who are not American citizens, but are leaders, diplomats or aides working at the **United Nations (UN)** or the **European Union (EU)**. Other countries with their own Communist Party organizations, will also use the American Mainstream Media, to fund their operations to produce wave-after-wave of propaganda. Many of these outside Communist Party organizations are located-in countries like Russia, China, Vietnam and from Marxists Millionaires and Billionaires in Hollywood, Business and Wall Street.[39,40]

Two of these organizations, which are internal to the United States of America, also feed the Mainstream American Media's enormous appetite to force Marxism down our throats, are the American Communist and Socialist Parties of America. (CPUSA/SPUSA)

The goal of the line media is this; to destabilize the country at United States enough to bring it into **Crisis** mode.

Chapter Six: Crisis-The American Proletariat Revolution

"Once the Socialists come to power, they will stay in power and keep the people fighting among themselves in order for the revolution to take place."

~Leonard Patterson~

Former Head of the Young Communist League (YCL)[1]

At this point during Ideological Subversion, the true legitimate bodies of both the government power structure, and social order, including Law and Order, Defense Systems, and relationships with our Allies overseas completely collapse!

It is here, where the United States of America, the last beacon of Freedom, Capitalism, and Free-Market Enterprise Competition cease to function as a nation.

Just prior to crisis mode, unknown "Committees" are established by Marxist-Leninists, who are **also not elected by the people** comes to the light.

These made up "Committees" will falsely proclaim that, **they are the ones who know how to lead a society**. They will publicly tell the people of United States, that if you rely on *them*, and put *them into power*, they would put an end to the Crisis.

In-reality, they don't know a damn thing about blowing up balloons at a birthday party, yet, they claim that know how to lead a society with a population of over 300-plus million people!

For example, the most recent country, as of this writing, (2019) that had gone through the Crisis stage, in which American Marxists are trying to create, is the South American country of **Venezuela**.[2,3]

Venezuela, a country with a population of over 28 million people, was once or oil rich and worldwide tourist attraction society, that was transformed from a Capitalistic society to a Socialist Police State.

In the early 1970s during the war worldwide Oil Crisis, created by OPEC, the Venezuelan currency and oil industry boomed, causing a massive decrease in unemployment for his people and the economy surged ahead.

By the 1980s, under the leadership of president **Dr. Jaime Lusinchi** (1924-2014), caused a sharp decrease in welfare spending and additional prosperity, throughout the country. At the same time, Venezuela's tourist industry boomed, when vacationers from across the world spent their money in the country for pleasure, further increasing the country economy.[4]

However, underneath the surface of this great economic prosperity, Marxists in that country we're well on his way to fundamentally transform Venezuela into a Socialist society.

In 1989, **Carlos Andreas "Cap" Perez**, was elected for second time in Venezuela. He served as President there for the first time between 1974-1979. During his second term in office, President Perez faced a Coup d'état in 1992, by the Marxist Organization, the **Revolutionary Bolivarian Movement (MBR-200)** led by-then **Colonel Hugo Chavez**.[5,6,7]

After his capture for staging the overthrow of the Perez Administration. Chavez was captured and jailed, serving two-years in prison. Upon his release, Chavez founded the **Fifth Republic Movement** (FRM) and was elected Venezuelan President in 1998 by a huge majority, Chavez was reelected twice, in 2000 and in 2006.[8,9,10]

Why is it important to know?

Easy.

Because what Venezuela did during the 1990s, is exactly the direction in which American Marxists and their subverted Liberal Dupes, are trying to take **this country**.

Venezuela, under President Carlos Perez, Marxist created fake movements, similar in nature to what the country of the United States is facing right now, by making such movements such as **Organizing for Action (OFA)**, led by **former Deputy White House Chief of Staff for Operations Jim Messina and former President Barack Obama** expedient and relevant to the social issues.[11,12,13]

Between 1989 to 1992, over 2000 people were killed and violent clashes, riots, and protests by the Venezuelan Marxist Elites with their country, with financial help from Communists at the United Nations (UN) and within the United States of America.[14]

After the two attempted coups, led by Chavez to overthrow the duty elected Venezuelan government, movements such as the Fifth Republican Movement, using the Communist Media as an avenue to subvert millions of Venezuelans to accept Marxist principles, began to cause massive chaos, "Crisis", when selected government officials were charged with corruption in kangaroo court trials.

Once Hugo Chavez won the presidency and came into power, him and his fellow Marxists began to implement "change", to the Venezuelan Economy. He led the fundamental transformation of Venezuela from a Capitalistic economic society, to a Socialism economic society, as advocated by Karl Marx and Friedrich Engels 150 years earlier.[14,15,16]

Soon, Venezuela's country was brought into a crisis mode when the government created a new constitution, was gave the judicial branch of government more power to legislate through the bench, thereby making the Venezuelan parliament ineffective.

The Chavez government, initiated Market Price Controls, conducted a hostile takeover of the country's oil industry, seized private property, and took over the Venezuelan banks. Chavez seized control of the country's healthcare system, implementing Universal Healthcare in the process, increased the country's welfare rolls and made the Military become the Law Enforcement agency of the country. To add on, Chavez stacked the Venezuelan Parliament with more Marxists, who only supported him and entered a $3 Billion-dollar Arms deal with Russia.

Pictured, Venezuelan Presidents Hugo Chavez (left) and Nicolas Maduro (right)

By 2008, Hugo Chavez nationalized the banks, signed a multibillion-dollar Telecommunication Satellite deal with China, and signed a Nuclear Disarmament deal with Russia. The following year the Venezuelan currency to Bolivar, plummet by 25% in value overnight, causing hyper-inflation of 133%, sparking riots between citizens opposing Chavez and the government's paramilitary forces.[17,18,19]

Prior to the death of Hugo Chavez, on March 5th, 2013 in Cuba from Cancer, the Bolivar was further devalued by another 17% against the US dollar, when the country was buying "priority imports" and another 50% for "non-essential" Import purchases. Such drastic devaluation of a country's currency ultimately made it worthless.

To counter react this severe devaluation of currency, **taxes in the country raise to a staggering 90% on the rich**, which increased government spending by $15,000,000,000 American dollars over 5 years, as the government begin to issue **Food Ration Cards** to the population. Following this, a series of natural disasters plagued Venezuela, such as floods, droughts, and the spread of diseases, begin to ravage the population. Because of this unforeseen emergencies, Venezuelan health care system began its own crisis from within to the point, that only those people, who originally required medical treatment as a last-minute need, were treated first, because of the severe shortage of medicine.[19,20,21,22]

Upon Chavez's death, his Vice-President, Nicolas Maduro become President of the Venezuela. Maduro, like his predecessor Hugo Chavez, was a trained Marxist-Leninist, who further moved the country even more into Socialism, and was a much bigger tyrant than Chavez ever was.

Maduro further increase the Venezuelan judicial powers tenfold, by giving them complete political power while seizing independent businesses institutions, forcing them to be regulated and fully controlled by the government.

The Maduro administration use its paramilitary forces and intelligence services to crack down on street protests, incarcerating dissenters and political opponents via military tribunals, who were charge with "**Insurrection**" or "**Counter-Revolutionary Activities**", then thrown in jail for years, without any family contact.[23,24,25]

Sounds familiar huh?

Since 2013, Venezuela's prison system became Soviet-style Gulags, where inmates were terrorized, beaten, sexually assaulted, sometimes killed, while the rest ended up living in unsanitary conditions or in solitary confinement. The country's jails and prison facilities were massively overcrowded, operated by corrupt management, who were controlled by the Maduro Government, headed by heavily-armed, brutal prison bosses.[26]

Government officials consistently harasses citizens, which occurs daily, as the country continues who have shortages of food, medicine and even daily hygiene products. There is such a shortage of regular goods and services for the people in Venezuela, that the Venezuelan people have-to wait in long lines, with their food ration cards in-hand, to obtain the little meat, bread and produce that the government gives them, which is supposed to last for a month.

Their government food rations have never lasted past two-weeks, for many. Instead of going hungry, while waiting for their next ration of food, people instead, rely on the Black Market to fulfill their needs in the meantime. However, relying on the Black Market to obtain fresh fruits and vegetables, meat and fish, while paying high-prices for such commodities, is risky business, because if the government finds out that people are participating in a Black Market, both the seller and the consumer can be arrested and jailed for years at a time.

Scores of Venezuelan people, line-up at a Pharmacy-Prescription store to receive personal hygiene products.

(Courtesy of Human Rights Watch)

The shortage of food is so enormous, that the Venezuelan people have resorted to eating out of garbage cans, garbage trucks, zoo animals, stay cats and dogs, rats and even birds!

Personal hygiene products such as soap toothpaste other hygienic products are not only rationed but once the country has obtained such novel tees, there are long lines of people waiting to obtain these products which sometimes end up in major fights and confrontations. **Electricity is ration, as Venezuela's inflation have risen to a staggering 1,600% since 2013.**[27,28,29,30]

Three alarming scenes from the "Socialist Paradise" of Venezuela. Food shortages have led to people killing zoo animals for meat to feed their families (top, left), to eating out of garbage cans (top, right) to looking at empty store shelves.

In 2016, the Infant Mortality Rate increased 30% in recent years, while the Women Maternal Mortality Rate has reached a mind-boggling 65%. The population has taken killing eat anything even in the capital city of Caracas.

Yet, Marxists in America want this country, to travel down the same road as Venezuela has done, all based-on the lie of "equality", "fairness", "civil rights", and "social justice".

Insane isn't it.

Once Crisis mode has commenced in the United States, so-called "Revolutionary Committees" will be formed, similar in scope and function to Venezuela 's **Operation People's Liberation (OPL)** committee formed under Hugo Chavez.[31]

These invented and made-up "Revolutionary Committees" and "Czars", will be granted the Power of Judgment, the Power of Execution, the Power of Legislation, and the supreme Power of the Courts. If such powers are denied to them, especially by those who are in opposition to them, the revolutionary committees will take their power by force, using their own paramilitary forces!

A sample of such made up committees and Czars, was seen starting in 2009, after the Inauguration of the 44th U.S. President, Marxist-Democrat Barack Hussein Obama.

During his 8-year tenure in office, Committees, Czars or in this case "Special Representatives" were appointed to positions of power in the Federal Government, which totaled 38. These new positions in the Federal Government, were not accountable to Congress, not accountable to the Courts or accountable to anybody else except the President himself!

A listing of these positions is annotated in the index pages in the back of the book.[32,33,34]

When crisis mode begins in this country, the entire United States Economic Structure will begin to collapse, because it has become unsustainable!

There are two main areas in which the United States of America will come into Crisis;[35]

A Civil War

A Foreign Invasion

If Marxists, their propagandists and their Useful Idiot Liberal Dupes bring the country into Crisis, an all-out bloody and violent revolution will take place on all our streets, cities, towns and States in America.

Law and order with no longer exist, our national sovereignty and border with Mexico, will be over ran with Illegal Foreign-born Aliens, who sole purpose is not to assimilate into American culture, but to destroy her economic system.

Such invaders will also murder and kill U.S. Citizens in cold-blood, while those coming from the Middle Eastern countries of Syria, Palestine, Jordan, Iran, Afghanistan, Yemen, Somalia and others will replace America's power and social structure with **"Sharia Law"**.[36]

Civil War

The main objective with Marxists, their Dupes and Propaganda Machine, is to divide the people and turn them against each other from within.[37]

Using the unelected Marxist media as a vehicle, which comprises of half-baked, non-reality living Journalists, Hollywood elites, these people are tasked to instill hatred, fear and intimidation to their American audiences.

For the Civil War to take place, once the country's social structure has become severely divided on American soil, this conflagration will be in a form of a massive Race War!

The people must be divided by Race, Gender, Culture, Economic, Culture, Politically, Socially, and by age. For an all-out Civil War or "American Proletariat Revolution" to happen, all Races will be pitted against each other.

This division of the populace is also extended to pitting the Old versus the Young.

What was once a time, where the Younger Generation of Americans were taught to respect their Elders and learn from the latter, has been made irrelevant. For the younger generation, who have been subverted by Marxists, the Older Generation of Americans, who are more patriotic then the newer generation, represent authority. So, in the Younger American generations' mind, those who have authority over them need to be destroyed or "just go away."

Of course, during Demoralization, and Destabilization, in-order to bring the country into Crisis, Marxists have subverted the younger generation, that the Older Generations of Americans is no longer valid and that the newer generation is better than the latter.

The young people in America, no matter what Race, Gender or Culture, would no longer have any respect for the old!

Of course, this comes at a price.

The Young versus the Old will become so prevalent, that in many instances, both will begin to harbor resentment and animosity towards each other, to the point where outright physical comfort confrontations between them will happen and sometimes such physical confrontations may end up deadly.

Also, for the Civil War between U.S. Citizens began to come to light, Communists and their propaganda machine, have-to pit Genders and Sexual Orientation populations against each other.

Communists in positions of power and prestige, right along with their Media lapdogs, will create agitation campaigns, which will pit Men against Women, Heterosexuals against Homosexuals, Transvestites against both Men and Women, who's sexual orientation is in social conflict with the latter.

Communist Front Groups, such as the LBGTQ Movement, #METOO! Movement and other Feminist Movement organizations will attempt to pit Lesbians against Heterosexuals, Homosexuals against Heterosexuals, and Transvestites against both biologically born Men and Women. This will be done using the mantra of **"Gender Equality"** or **"Gender Inequity"**.

Laurel Hubbard, 39-year-old Transgender, won the Female International Weightlifting Title in March 2017 (left) and Dr. Rachel McKinnon (right, center), was the first Transgender to win a Woman's Cycling Event in October 2018.

(Photos courtesy of The Gateway Pundit)

Texas Transgender Female, Mack Beggs competes and wins against Female Wrestler in 2018.

(Courtesy of Washington Times)

Propagandist will create false narratives in which, those who are so-called "**transitioning**" from Males into Females, should compete against biologically-born Females in sporting events. Anybody who opposes such lunacy will be labeled as a "homophobe", "Xenophobe", in which such opposition is a violation of the Transitioning Male's "Civil Rights".

Not only that such advocation is a big lie but is delusional at best.

Besides the obvious biological and physical differences between Males and Females, these "**Males Transitioning to Females**", are *__still Males__* and they will always have an advantage over Females, in competitive Sports.

But Communists does not give a damn about that!

As a matter of fact, Marxists and their Useful Idiot Liberal Dupes, will force you to believe that you are not born biologically as you appear to be! These Propagandists will also make you believe, that even at a very young age, that you are born as whoever or whatever you want to be, regardless or not you were born biologically Male or Female!

This is sick!

Communist Propagandists in the Media will also change the language as to determine what sexual orientation one is as well.

Terms like "Cisgender" will become mainstream. Communists will define, that a Cisgender is a person who Sex (Gender) is assigned at birth! These same propagandists will invent other terminologies to define who they want to define, to further divide the country and bring it into Crisis.[38,39]

For example, Marxists in Hollywood and their Useful Idiot of Actors, Actresses and Entertainers, will create reality shows, movies, and drama series, to pit the social differences between Genders.

Television shows such as "**Basketball Wives**", clearly shows African- American and Hispanic Women, who are married to actual NBA players or former players or portrayed as having "**drama-filled lives**", which causes each other to have social and physical confrontations, usually over material things. Programs such as the "**Real-World**", "**The Hills**", "**Laguna Beach**", and the "**Jersey Shore**", are examples of television shows, that make the viewer believe that the role of Actors and Actresses, along with their social disorders or real and factual, when in-reality they are fake and scripted. The after-mentioned programming is created to specifically target audiences who age range is between 12 and 34.

Communist also target the specific age groups, to subvert both Male and Female Teens and Early-Adults, to program their minds into accepting Socialism, because they are susceptible to being dissatisfied with their environment, or disordered behavior.[40,41]

During the Crisis stage, there will be an ever-increasing distinction of absolute hatred and discontent levied against those who are considered "wealthy" and those who are considered "poor".

What distinguish between rich and poor during Crisis mode, becomes irrelevant.

For the Proletariat Revolution to start on American streets, Marxists instilled in the populace with so much venomous hate towards those who have become so successful to increase their quality of life, that the subverted population will conduct criminal acts against those who have more material items than they own. Such acts include Burglary, Stealing, Carjacking, Home Invasions, Armed Robbery on innocent people, to include Intimidation, Stalking, Physical Confrontations and outright Homicide!

Foreign Invasion

One of the many so-called "Migrant Caravans" attempting to overwhelm the U.S.-Mexico Border in 2018.

(Courtesy Fox News Channel)

When it comes to Foreign Invasion, you can see it for yourself clearly, as of this writing; and it's happening right this very instance at a Southern Border with Mexico.

These "**Invaders**" will come through the U.S. Southern Border in so large of numbers, that it will be almost entirely impossible to stem the flow of the Foreign-born persons from coming into America.

One can see it clearly when you look at the Marxist propagandized Media, The **United Nations High Commissioner of Refugees (UNHCR)**, Communist Politicians in both the Democrat and Republican Parties, Communist Front Groups, like La Raza and the Hollywood Elites, advocate and finance large "Caravans" of migrants, who are actually Invaders, who originate from Central America, overwhelming our border with Mexico.[42,43,44]

However, some of them are not just from Central America, who are illegally coming into this country, but they originate from other Third-World nations across the Globe, from;

Mexico *Vietnam*

China *Syria*

Honduras	*Jordan*
Nicaragua	*Iraq*
Costa Rica	*Afghanistan*
Guatemala	*Iran*
Pakistan	*Yemen*
Somalia	*Bangladesh*
Egypt	*Libya*

Understand, the marks in America and throughout the world or financing these groups of foreign Nationals to further destroy the United States and bring it into crisis.

Criminal elements such as **Mara Salvatrucha (MS-13)**, **La Eme (Mexican Mafia)**, Radical Islamic Terrorist Organizations, such as the **Islamic State of Iraq and Syria (ISIS)**, **Al Qaeda**, **Muslim Brotherhood**, **Hamas** and many others. Such criminal elements will use the US-Mexican Border to funnel drugs, Illegal Aliens, move stolen guns, stolen property, other gang members to render Law Enforcement at the border ineffective.

These Illegal Invaders will also take advantage of our porous and open-ended Immigration Laws, to take advantage of, so that such Illegals can not only seek Asylum here, but also bring others into to the country as well, such as family members and the like, called "**Chain Migration**".

Understand, that the-majority of these Illegal Aliens invading our southern border, are not here to assimilate into the American Culture, but to destroy the social fabric of the country, <u>**bring it into Crisis mode, by fundamentally crashing the U.S. Economy**</u>. Such invaders also would do a second thing and that is to add to the population, a new underclass of Proletariats in America, to keep the Marxist-Leninists in power and use them to formulate the Proletarian Revolution on our soil.

One of many Central-American "Migrant Caravans", assembling to make the trek from Honduras to the U.S. Border with Mexico, sponsored by the United Nations. (Photo courtesy of the United Nations Migrant Agency)

By crashing the United States Economic System, mass chaos will ensue, where American citizens, Naturalized American citizens will protest in mass numbers, against the foreign invaders, which are duly financed by the world-wide Communist Order. Such clashes will also resort to American Citizens taking the law into their own hands, in their attempt to help Law Enforcement Agencies stem the flow of these invaders. This action could lead to violent confrontations between the Illegals and American Citizens, causing numerous injuries, deaths and chaos.

This is exactly what these Communists in America want!

As for the Criminal Elements, their purpose is to cause mass chaos in America, by totally collapsing the U.S. Law and Order system. Their job is to overpower the Border Patrol (BP), Customs, Immigration and Enforcement (ICE), Federal Marshals, County Sheriff Departments, who are located along the border and Local Law Enforcement personnel. The criminal elements such as the Mexican Mafia, MS-13, Islamic Jihadists will do so to the point, where Law Enforcement Agencies, will not have enough resources to stem the flow of drugs, Illegals, Human Sex Trafficking, Gang Members from infiltrating American cities.[45,46,47,48]

Communist Politicians, such as Governors, State Legislature, Mayors, City Councils and the like, will proclaim their metropolitan areas as **"Sanctuary Cities"** or **"Sanctuary States"**, where they will give aid and comfort to the Illegal Criminal Elements and assist such Foreign Invaders to overwhelm the country's welfare system. Which will give them Government Entitlements, where the Taxpayer's money will be allotted to them, causing the economy not to grow, but increase into staggering debt!

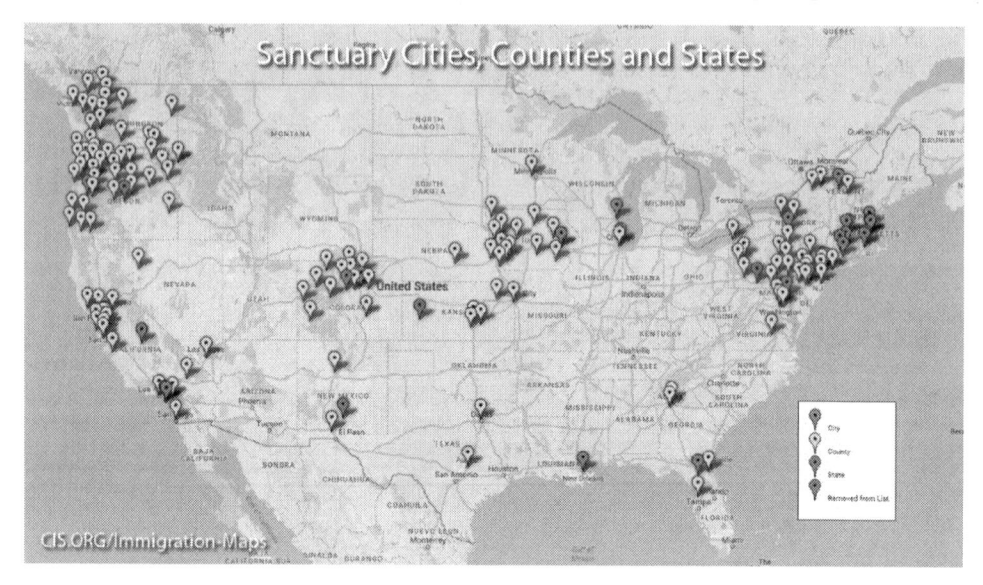

Sanctuary Cities, Counties and States

How could this happen?

As of this writing, the population of the United States of America stood at 328.4 million people. Currently we have racked up over $22 trillion in debt, over $125 trillion dollars in Unfunded Liabilities, with only 122.3 million Taxpayers paying the bill.

Furthermore, when the projected population of the country adding illegal immigration, Birth and Death Rate Replacement, is expected to reach 441 million people by 2065, adding on to the newest immigrants being placed on the welfare rolls, the collapse of the American Economy is inevitable, unless something is done right now! At this point, the economy of the United States will be unsustainable.[50,51,52,53,54]

Marxists want this to occur, for the simple fact that if the U.S. Economy is killed, this will bring the country into Crisis, where they will overthrow the duly elected president in a ***Coup D'état***, which will further bring on the Proletariat Revolution by violence.

Once this occurs, the United States of America will cease to exist!

Just like what happened in Venezuela, once a Coup de eta is successful in America, the made-up Committees and Czars, along with the Deep State, which really exist at the present, further advance their agenda will in at the next stage up on the fundamental transformation of the United States of America.

The enactment of socialism throughout the country.

Once a Coup d eta is successful during Crisis mode, chaotic civil unrest, anarchy, and a violent revolution, which would have started, will eventually need to be permanently put down. Because a country cannot reform itself into the image of Karl Marx and Frederick Engels, where Full Socialism needed to be put in place, by the new Masters of the new ***Soviet States of America***!

When the new leaders of **Soviet States of America (SSA)** have taken power, stability of society have-to be enforced throughout the country! The new Communist leaders of Soviet America will form and use their own paramilitary forces, who have become loyal to the new leaders, to gain control of the people. Once this has been established, the final stage of Ideological Subversion will begin; it is called the period of **Normalization.**

Chapter Seven: Normalization-The United Soviet States of America (USSA)

"To choose one's victim, to prepare one's plans minutely, to stake an implacable vengeance, and then go to bed...there is nothing sweeter in the world."   ~Joseph Stalin~

The term **_Normalization_**, within itself, was created during the 1940s, 50s and 1960s, as a cynical expression coined by Soviet Union KGB Propagandists.

Normalization was declared by the Warsaw Pact troops from the Soviet Union, invaded Poland, Bulgaria, East Germany and Hungary during that era, which was led by Alexander Dubcek.[1]

In this phase of ideological subversion, all an archaeal violence must come to an end in the new Soviet States of America.

Former Soviet KGB Propagandist and Journalist Yuri Bezmenov stated this in-regards to the Normalization process;

"**_It can last indefinitely!_**"[2]

Here, the self-appointed rules of society, the made-up Committees and Czars, will no longer be needed, because their job to transform America into a Venezuelan-Soviet Union-type Socialist society is now complete.

Every Communist Front Group, Civil Rights organizations, both the Communist and Socialist Parties of what was then, the United States of America, would need to be "**liquidated**" and/or "**purged**" from society, usually by violence if needed, which will be ordered by the new rulers of society.

The following is an inclusive list of organizations, Communist Front Groups, and Movements, along with their members and leaders, who will be targeted for liquidation by the new rulers of Soviet America;

The Communist Party of the United States (CPUSA)

The Socialist Party of the United States (SPUSA)

All Self-Appointed Committee and Czars

All Communist Front Groups to include;

    Black Lives Matter (BLM)

    Antifa

    LBGTQ Movement

    # Me Too! Movement

    Organizing for Action (OFA)

    Industrial Areas Foundation (IAF)

    AFL-CIO and all its Public Service Union affiliates

    CPUSA's tentacle groups, such as the Democratic Socialists of America (DSA)

    SPUSA tentacle groups, such as the Young Communist League

    All Marxist-Leninist in the Media, including CEOs and News Anchors of Television, and Radio Networks

    All Marxist-Leninists in Academia, Business, Hollywood, and Humanitarian Foundations

    All Civil Rights Leaders and Civil Rights Groups, such as National Association for the Advancement of Colored People (NAACP), the American Civil Liberties Union (ACLU), the Southern Poverty Law Center (SPLC), National Action Network (NAN), the Rainbow Coalition, Council on American Religious Discrimination (CARD), Council on American-Islamic Relations (CAIR), Center for

American Progress (CAP), La Raza (the Race) and many other civil rights groups.

All Religious Clergy throughout all religions

All Marxists occupying positions of power in Congress and other places with the federal government

All Climate Change "Scientists"

All Environmental Justice groups

All Earth Justice groups

All Feminist groups

and All opposition to Socialism and opposition to the new rulers of the Soviet States of America!

<u>**Unless the above members in the affirmation groups pledge allegiance to the new Soviet states of American government, these persons will be executed violently come by firing squads, public executions, car bombs or simply come up "missing", And never heard from ever again!**</u>

Paraphrasing former KGB Operative, Yuri Bezmenov;

"They will be killed off like cockroaches."

The Soviet American government will not explain to the public as to what had happened to them these groups, or ever mention the reason(s) of why the above-mentioned persons that they have targeted are no longer with us. [3,4,5]

Such incidents have happened to many times within the past one-hundred-plus years.

In July 1918, months after the Bolshevik Revolution took place in Russia, operating under the orders of President Vladimir Lenin, the Soviet Secret Police, the **Cheka**, began their murderous rampage against those who either helped the revolution take place months before or dissenters to the Socialist Government.

The Cheka began to investigate, arrest, adjudicating and openly executing people in public, who have become disillusioned with the glories of "a socialist paradise" being instilled throughout the country. Just in July alone, over 500 people were tried in Kangaroo Courts on trumped-up charges, convicted and faced firing squads, who killed such dissenters, while burying them on open-graves![6,7,8]

Another great example of such travesty on innocent people, occurred under Soviet Dictator Joseph Stalin between 1928 and 1938.

As Stalin and his henchmen began to wipeout prosperous independent business owners and Peasant Farmers (Kulaks), he ordered the Cheka and the Soviet Army (Red Army) to use force to confiscate private property and annex such industries under the umbrella of the Socialist Government.

This operation known today as Stalin's "**First Five-Year Plan**", the Cheka and Army forces conducted unspeakable atrocities against their own people, killing over 1000 people in the process. As for the Kulaks, Joseph Stalin wanted to eliminate them entirely, by using genocidal liquidation!

Sensing this action, the Kulaks began to burn everything they owned to the ground; houses, cars, livestock, crops, towns and villages, as they fled on foot towards the Caucasus Mountains.

Unfortunately for many, the Kulaks were caught by Red Army forces, who not only used their own rifles and pistols to kill, but whole towns and villages were wiped out using artillery rounds to blast the homes and groups of fleeing Men, Women and Children.

At the end, Joseph Stalin, one of the many Marxist heroes idolized by the American Communist and Socialist Left, was responsible for the murdering of over 50,000 people!

Who says that something like this can happen here in the United States of America, during the period of Normalization?

It can and it has happened over-and-over again in over twenty countries who have tried to implement Socialism into their societies, including China, North Korea, Cuba and Venezuela!

Just like Joseph Stalin and Vladimir Lenin, this new Soviet American Government will be usher in a genocidal society, rife with corruption, murders, with the conviction and imprisonment of millions of people.

Because they know intimately know, that the same people who were both active members or supported such organizations, which brought this country into crisis, will become the biggest dissenters and opposition to the new Socialist Power Structure operated by the new Socialist States of American Government.

Some of the target people, the persons whose job was to push the United States into Crisis, will be dragged in-front of Kangaroo Courts, with made-up charges levied against them after their arrest, by Paramilitary Forces. These glorious Civil Rights Leaders, Marxist-Leninists and Social Justice Warrior Activists **will not be given their Miranda Rights!**

Plus, these so-called "beautiful Civil Rights Leaders", will have no legal representation to defend such baseless charges, no nothing. The only Plea they will be able give is Guilty or Innocent.

Whether there are found guilty or innocent, it doesn't matter to the new Socialist American Government! Because it will up to the Kangaroo Courts, who are, by-the-way, are loyal servants to the new rulers in power, and newly released convicted criminals themselves, are the ones to judge whether such people will be sentenced to execution or jailed indefinitely![9,10,11]

As for the jails, they will be operated like the former Soviet Gulags, where they will be overcrowded, unsanitary conditions, little food, water, as they live in solitary confinement 24-hours a day, with no walls, no television, no internet, no outside communications, inside cells that are infested with body fleas, rats and roaches![12,13,14]

The jails mentioned above, currently are in existence today and is not part of the current prison system of America; but they are called today **FEMA camps**, and they will be used to house any and all dissenters charged with so-called "Counter-Revolutionary Activities", or other charges made up to sequester people who goes against the new Soviet American Government.

It will be at this time, that the Marxists and their Useful Idiot Liberals Dupes will finally began to enjoy all the glories of Socialist Equality!

Scary isn't it?

There is more.

Pictured above, Chinese Communists executing those who helped Mao Zedong come to power in the 1950s.

Pictured above, Map of FEMA Regions around the United States (left) and FEMA Railroad Cars (right), which will be used to transport Marxists and dissenters of the new Socialist Government in America to such FEMA gulag-type camps.

Homosexuals, Lesbians, Transvestites, Queer, and Cisgenders will be publicly executed or thrown in detention centers as well, where they will be tortured, raped, beaten savagely, are simply killed via public executions ***because*** of their Sexual Orientation.

Hollywood Actors, Actresses, Entertainers and Marxist Elites who operate the Unelected Media, would be tried and convicted in the same after-mentioned Kangaroo Courts and they will also be jailed in overcrowded FEMA camp detention centers with the same poor sanitation, insect-infested places, **unless they pledge allegiance to the new Soviet American Government!**

Their wealth will be confiscated, every bit of their assets seized by government officials, their families broken apart, whom they will never be seen again, as these elites they go through the new unfair courts and be jailed without due process.

As a matter of fact, World History has shown, then when a country falls to Socialism, these same Hollywood Actors and Actresses, will be housed in the same places and the same jail cells, **with real criminals**! The same criminals, Murderers, Rapists, Gang Members and Sexual Predators who they not only try to imitate on film, but advocated for, when they assisted and supported to Demoralize, Destabilize and brought the country into Crisis.[15,16,17,18,19]

Church Leaders, Ministers, Bishops and Clergymen and women, who have pushed the poisonous lies of Liberation and Black Liberation Theologies, will either be imprisoned in FEMA Camps as well or purged from society altogether.

As previously mentioned, their Houses of Worship will be seized by the Soviet America Government Officials, which will either be vandalized, or completely-destroyed by purposely set explosions and fires, or the buildings will be razed via the wrecking ball. Many of them will be converted into bureaucratic office buildings!

As for the Foreign-Born, they will be sent to "**FEMA Camp Zones**", via bus, plane or train, by force and violence to populate new cities near the existing FEMA camps. Their property their personal possessions will be seized by government officials, their families broken up as previously mentioned, and legal/traditional Marriages will be ruled by the government as being ***null and void***![20,21]

Believe it or not, American citizens will be segregated by Race and Economic classes! Those in a new Soviet States of America will be sent to special designated "**Living Zones**", because States and State boundaries would no longer exist. There may or may not be Cities or Towns in the new

America, but there will be no borders; such things will no longer exist, hence the term "**Open Society**".

Blacks would be segregated in one part of town, Whites will be in another and Hispanics will be relegated to live in "ghettos" or "barrios" as well, because each of these new living zones will be monitored 24/7 by armed guards, and para-militia forces surrounded by walls and bobbed-wire. Some of these neighborhoods will be patrolled by armored personnel carriers, tanks and Mine-Resistant vehicles, laden with military troops.

Photos of SWAT forces evacuate a family in the Watertown area of Boston Massachusetts, while searching for Boston Marathon Bomber Dzhokhar A. Tsarnaev, April 2013 and Paramilitary Forces putting down Anti-government protests in Caracas, Venezuela. (Courtesy of WBUR and Human Rights Watch)

Water, Gas or Electric Utilities will be limited, scarce and rationed, all private property will be seized, even by force and will be given to the almighty rules of the new society.

History has already taught us, that Communist Dictators have went so far to the point, where a new class of people was created, who will be given 'priority' over goods and serves. By doing so, this new class of people, called Bureaucrats, will be given an unlimited supply of Water, Gas, Electric Utilities and even healthcare, where the rest of the population of the new society called Soviet America, will be rationed.

For example, Joseph Stalin after the Great Purge conducted between 1935-1938, created the Bureaucratic Class of citizens in Russia, where by law, benefited off the backs of the workers.

Called a "Spoils System", Stalin bestowed favors to those who were totally inline with his ideology, by allowing to shop at closed-to-the-public distribution centers, which had great quantity of supplies, which were never intended to be distributed to the "working class".

The same bureaucrats also had top priority in their choice of dwellings, the amount of land they can be purchased, unlimited supply of luxuries, jewels, high-end cars from all over the world, special holidays and special high-quality of education for their children. Education which was never intended for the rest of the population.[22]

Everyone else will work with little or no pay in industries who have their own interest and loyalty to the new Soviet American Government. There will be a steady work 24 hours a day, 7 days a week, in manufacturing companies, that will give out their own form of punishment to those workers who have not complied with the company rules or regulations! There will be no Union Representation, no Collective Bargaining, no nothing to represent "Worker's Rights"!

In simpler terms, the labor force in Soviet America will be equivalent to modern day Slavery.

And, you better like it!

The people will be issued "Ration Cards", which Adults depending on age, will go to the nearest Market, which has been sanctioned by the new Soviet American Government, to receive their "fair share" of Meat, Bread and Produce.

They will get just enough rations to live-on for two-weeks by the government standards, which is **_never enough_** to live on. Those on Ration Cards would either turn to the Black Market or turn to a stealing food for those who have it, which could land them in prison if they're caught. Those caught stealing food would **not have** a court trial to plead their case, and therefore regulated into any one of the country's Gulag-type prisons.

In the words of **Vladimiro Rocha**, a Human Rights Activist and former Havana Cuba native, who was held in one of Cuba's "Gulag-type" Prisons, for five years, had this to say about living in a pure Socialist country;

"Here, people get thrown in Prison for anything...If you Kill a cow to feed your family, you go to jail. That's part of the government's method to maintain control of the population".[23,24]

Pictured above, overcrowded prison cell in Venezuela (left) and a Cuban Prisoner locked behind bars in single cells (right).

Since Human Beings are different at require different needs, the Socialist Government of America, during the Normalization period, will dictate how much each person shall receive; hence the Black-Market system will become prominent in that society.

However, those persons who have pledge allegiance to the new Socialist Government, will receive priority in obtaining the best made products first. After the what would be called, the "**Socialist Elites**" received the best-made products, then everyone else, who are constantly living and working to death, going hungry because the lack of food, or being constantly sick because of the lack of health care, will receive what goods are left, last.

You can see this for yourself when you look at socialist countries of;

Angola

Barbados

Bolivia

Congo

China

Ecuador

El Salvador

Ethiopia

Guinea-Bissau

Greece

Mauritius

Mozambique

Mexico

Nepal

North Korea

Nicaragua

People's Republic of Bangladesh

Saint Vincent

Grenada

Suriname

Tanzania

Uruguay

Venezuela

Zambia

Peoples Democratic Republic of Laos

Socialist Republic of Vietnam

During the initial period of Normalization, due to the massive reduction of goods and services, utilities, healthcare and disease eradication, Socialist countries always experience a large famine first, which grips the country at the beginning.

When Russia fell to Communism after the Bolshevik Revolution, under the dictatorship of Vladimir Lenin, a large famine outbreak occurred between 1921 and 1922, resulting in the deaths of 5,000,000 people. Another famine took place in Russia under the dictatorship of Joseph Stalin, occurred between 1932 and 1933, which plagued the Soviet Countries of Ukraine, the Northern Caucasus, Volga Region, Kazakhstan, the South Urals and Western Siberia. This famine resulted an additional 3.5-7.5 million people dead.[25,26,27,28]

Picture of a Russian Family suffering from the Famine of 1921.

(Courtesy of Research Gate)

Other famines which were directly associated with Marxist Ideology of Karl Marx during the 20th century include;

China- 1958 to 1962 under the dictatorship of Mao Zedong resulting in 10-30 million deaths[29,30]

North Korea- 1995 to 1999, 5 million people died due to governmental policy and flooding rains

Soviet Union- 1946 to 1947, two million people died from drought conditions and Communist policies under Joseph Stalin, when he re-enforced the act of agriculture collectivism after World War Two[31,32]

Cambodia- 1979, 1.5 to 2 million Cambodians died from famine under the dictatorship of Pol Pot, which resulted in the brutal genocide of the population known as the Khmer Rouge

Ethiopia- 1972 to 1973/ 1984 to 1985, 60,000 deaths/400,000 deaths

Somalia- 1991 to 1992, 300,000 deaths due to famine and Socialist policies

Democratic Republic of the Congo- 1998 to 2004, 3.8 million people

West Africa- 2006 to 2007, 10 million people died from famine

Somalia- 2011, 250,000 people died from famine

As stated earlier, the Normalization period after United States of America has fell to Socialism and become the Soviet States of America, this Normalization period can last indefinitely!

A Chinese Teen and his Mother, suffering through Communist Dictator Mao Zedong's "Great Leap Forward" Famine crisis of 1959.

This means, that what was once the United States, the country where unlimited opportunity to succeed, the freedom to do what you want, when you want, with Freedom of Speech, Freedom of Religion, and to do what you want to do, without an oppressing government telling you to do anything, which you desire, as granted by God, will become a **Socialist Police State**.

A State where only the **Collective Few**, will control the entire population, by force and intimidation using paramilitary forces and Gestapo-type surveillance, in-order to profit and benefit of those who are suffering because of the lack of food, medicine and basic hygiene.

Once Normalization has taken place, the United States of America as it was founded by our Forefathers, will no longer exists and will never exist again! Because, sadly, **<u>once you become a Socialist Nation, you can never ever revert-back to a Capitalistic Society, no matter how long it will take, how many lives have-to be lost without shedding more blood and taking of innocent lives.</u>**

Just the thought of the United States becoming a Socialist hellhole like Venezuela, Cuba, North Korea and other places, should have you very concern and scared to death, that your freedom can be easily extinguished that quickly.

The 40th United States of America President, Republican Ronald Wilson Reagan (1911-2004), stated this during his two-terms as Chief Executive of America;

"Freedom is never more than one generation away from extinction. We didn't pass it to our children in the bloodstream. It must be fought for, protected, and handed on for them to do the same."[33]

Therefore, it is intuitive for the American people to fully understand and comprehend, that what is written in this book is not hyperbole but is a fact!

<u>*Ideological Subversion is real*</u>, and it is happening right here, right now on the streets of America! If we do not wake up in time and defeat the Marxist Propagandists, Marxist Elites on every level of society, then the United States of America (USA) will become the Soviet States of America (SSA). It will be then, you can kiss your freedom goodbye and say hello to your oppression.

GOALS OF MARXISM:

1. Destroy the Family
2. Destroy Private Property
3. Destroy Religion
4. Destroy the Nation

Index

Common Core Standards Example

Dear Parents,   10-1-12

We wanted to send you a "Common Core – Parent Cheat Sheet" to help you understand the processes in which your child is solving problems in math class. Remember, the philosophy of the Common Core standards is to create a deeper understanding of numbers and their values to help build a foundation for future math skills. The idea is not to just "do it" but to know "how and why" we do it. Please let either of us know if you have any questions as we are both working together with all of our students to help meet their specific needs.

Mrs. ▓▓▓▓▓▓▓

Old Language	New Language
word problem	math situation
carry the one	regroup ten ones as a ten
borrow	take a ten and regroup it as ten ones
*add	increase
*subtract	decrease
*more than / fewer than	compare
How do you know?	evidence

*Please note that we do still use "add/subtract/more than, less than", but we interchange it with the new language you see listed beside each of these words to create a deeper understanding.

The old way to solve an addition problem:	The new way to solve an addition math situation:
$$\begin{array}{r} 62 \\ +26 \\ \hline 88 \end{array}$$	One way... expanded form: $$\begin{array}{r} 60 + 2 \\ 20 + 6 \\ \hline 80 + 8 = 88 \end{array}$$

Please turn over...

	A second way... **base ten block symbols:**
	(IIIIII xx) (II xxxxx x) ↓ ↓ 80 8 = 88
	A third way... **place value:** 6 tens 2 ones 2 tens 6 ones ―――――――――― 8 tens 8 ones = 88
	A fourth way... **a number line:** 62 + 26 (20+6) (88) ←—•⌒⌒—•⌒—•⌒⌒⌒⌒—→ 62 72 82 88

The old way to solve a more than/fewer than problem:	The new way to solve a comparing math situation:
There were 12 red cars and 7 blue cars. How many fewer blue cars were there than red cars? 7 + ☐ = 12 or 5 fewer 12 − 7 = ☐ blue cars.	→ ⌒1 ⌒2 ⌒3 ⌒4 ⌒5 ←—(7)—8—9—10—11—(12)—→ 5 fewer

The Democrat Party's "Green New Deal" Legislation

PAT19116   S.L.C.

Edward J. Markey

116TH CONGRESS
1ST SESSION   **S. RES. ____**

Recognizing the duty of the Federal Government to create a Green New Deal.

IN THE SENATE OF THE UNITED STATES

for himself and

Mr. MARKEY submitted the following resolution; which was referred to the Committee on _____

Mr. Merkley
Mr. Sanders
Ms. Gillibrand
Ms. Harris
Ms. Warren
Ms. Hirono
Mr. Wyden
Mr. Blumenthal
Mr. Booker
Ms. Klobuchar

RESOLUTION

Recognizing the duty of the Federal Government to create a Green New Deal.

Whereas the October 2018 report entitled "Special Report on Global Warming of 1.5 Cº" by the Intergovernmental Panel on Climate Change and the November 2018 Fourth National Climate Assessment report found that—

(1) human activity is the dominant cause of observed climate change over the past century;

(2) a changing climate is causing sea levels to rise and an increase in wildfires, severe storms, droughts, and other extreme weather events that threaten human life, healthy communities, and critical infrastructure;

(3) global warming at or above 2 degrees Celsius beyond pre-industrialized levels will cause—

(A) mass migration from the regions most affected by climate change;

(B) more than $500,000,000,000 in lost annual economic output in the United States by the year 2100;

(C) wildfires that, by 2050, will annually burn at least twice as much forest area in the western United States than was typically burned by wildfires in the years preceding 2019;

(D) a loss of more than 99 percent of all coral reefs on Earth;

(E) more than 350,000,000 more people to be exposed globally to deadly heat stress by 2050; and

(F) a risk of damage to $1,000,000,000,000 of public infrastructure and coastal real estate in the United States; and

(4) global temperatures must be kept below 1.5 degrees Celsius above pre-industrialized levels to avoid the most severe impacts of a changing climate, which will require—

(A) global reductions in greenhouse gas emissions from human sources of 40 to 60 percent from 2010 levels by 2030; and

(B) net-zero global emissions by 2050;

Whereas, because the United States has historically been responsible for a disproportionate amount of greenhouse gas emissions, having emitted 20 percent of global greenhouse gas emissions through 2014, and has a high technological capacity, the United States must take a leading role in reducing emissions through economic transformation;

Whereas the United States is currently experiencing several related crises, with—

(1) life expectancy declining while basic needs, such as clean air, clean water, healthy food, and adequate health care, housing, transportation, and education, are inaccessible to a significant portion of the United States population;

(2) a 4-decade trend of wage stagnation, deindustrialization, and anti-labor policies that has led to—

(A) hourly wages overall stagnating since the 1970s despite increased worker productivity;

(B) the third-worst level of socioeconomic mobility in the developed world before the Great Recession;

(C) the erosion of the earning and bargaining power of workers in the United States; and

(D) inadequate resources for public sector workers to confront the challenges of climate change at local, State, and Federal levels; and

(3) the greatest income inequality since the 1920s, with—

(A) the top 1 percent of earners accruing 91 percent of gains in the first few years of economic recovery after the Great Recession;

(B) a large racial wealth divide amounting to a difference of 20 times more wealth between the average white family and the average black family; and

(C) a gender earnings gap that results in women earning approximately 80 percent as much as men, at the median;

Whereas climate change, pollution, and environmental destruction have exacerbated systemic racial, regional, social, environmental, and economic injustices (referred to in this preamble as "systemic injustices") by disproportionately affecting indigenous peoples, communities of color, migrant communities, deindustrialized communities, depopulated rural communities, the poor, low-income workers, women, the elderly, the unhoused, people with disabilities, and youth (referred to in this preamble as "frontline and vulnerable communities");

Whereas, climate change constitutes a direct threat to the national security of the United States—

(1) by impacting the economic, environmental, and social stability of countries and communities around the world; and

(2) by acting as a threat multiplier;

Whereas the Federal Government-led mobilizations during World War II and the New Deal created the greatest middle class that the United States has ever seen, but many members of frontline and vulnerable communities were excluded from many of the economic and societal benefits of those mobilizations; and

Whereas the Senate recognizes that a new national, social, industrial, and economic mobilization on a scale not seen since World War II and the New Deal era is a historic opportunity—

(1) to create millions of good, high-wage jobs in the United States;

(2) to provide unprecedented levels of prosperity and economic security for all people of the United States; and

(3) to counteract systemic injustices: Now, therefore, be it

1 *Resolved,* That it is the sense of the Senate that—

(1) it is the duty of the Federal Government to create a Green New Deal—

 (A) to achieve net-zero greenhouse gas emissions through a fair and just transition for all communities and workers;

 (B) to create millions of good, high-wage jobs and ensure prosperity and economic security for all people of the United States;

 (C) to invest in the infrastructure and industry of the United States to sustainably meet the challenges of the 21st century;

 (D) to secure for all people of the United States for generations to come—

  (i) clean air and water;

  (ii) climate and community resiliency;

  (iii) healthy food;

  (iv) access to nature; and

  (v) a sustainable environment; and

 (E) to promote justice and equity by stopping current, preventing future, and repairing historic oppression of indigenous peoples, communities of color, migrant communities, deindustrialized communities, depopulated rural communities, the poor, low-income workers, women, the elderly, the unhoused, people with disabilities, and youth (referred to in this resolution as "frontline and vulnerable communities");

(2) the goals described in subparagraphs (A) through (E) of paragraph (1) (referred to in this resolution as the "Green New Deal goals") should be accomplished through a 10-year national mobilization (referred to in this resolution as the "Green New Deal mobilization") that will require the following goals and projects—

(A) building resiliency against climate change-related disasters, such as extreme weather, including by leveraging funding and providing investments for community-defined projects and strategies;

(B) repairing and upgrading the infrastructure in the United States, including—

(i) by eliminating pollution and greenhouse gas emissions as much as technologically feasible;

(ii) by guaranteeing universal access to clean water;

(iii) by reducing the risks posed by climate impacts; and

(iv) by ensuring that any infrastructure bill considered by Congress addresses climate change;

(C) meeting 100 percent of the power demand in the United States through clean, renewable, and zero-emission energy sources, including—

(i) by dramatically expanding and upgrading renewable power sources; and

(ii) by deploying new capacity;

(D) building or upgrading to energy-efficient, distributed, and "smart" power grids, and ensuring affordable access to electricity;

(E) upgrading all existing buildings in the United States and building new buildings to achieve maximum energy efficiency, water efficiency, safety, affordability, comfort, and durability, including through electrification;

(F) spurring massive growth in clean manufacturing in the United States and removing pollution and greenhouse gas emissions from manufacturing and industry as much as is technologically feasible, including by expanding renewable energy manufacturing and investing in existing manufacturing and industry;

(G) working collaboratively with farmers and ranchers in the United States to remove pollution and greenhouse gas emissions from the agricultural sector as much as is technologically feasible, including—

 (i) by supporting family farming;

 (ii) by investing in sustainable farming and land use practices that increase soil health; and

 (iii) by building a more sustainable food system that ensures universal access to healthy food;

(H) overhauling transportation systems in the United States to remove pollution and greenhouse gas emissions from the transportation sector as much as is technologically feasible, including through investment in—

 (i) zero-emission vehicle infrastructure and manufacturing;

 (ii) clean, affordable, and accessible public transit; and

 (iii) high-speed rail;

(I) mitigating and managing the long-term adverse health, economic, and other effects of pollution and climate change, including by providing funding for community-defined projects and strategies;

(J) removing greenhouse gases from the atmosphere and reducing pollution by restoring natural ecosystems through proven low-tech solutions that increase soil carbon storage, such as land preservation and afforestation;

(K) restoring and protecting threatened, endangered, and fragile ecosystems through locally appropriate and science-based projects that enhance biodiversity and support climate resiliency;

(L) cleaning up existing hazardous waste and abandoned sites, ensuring economic development and sustainability on those sites;

(M) identifying other emission and pollution sources and creating solutions to remove them; and

(N) promoting the international exchange of technology, expertise, products, funding, and services, with the aim of making the United States the international leader on climate action, and to help other countries achieve a Green New Deal;

(3) a Green New Deal must be developed through transparent and inclusive consultation, collaboration, and partnership with frontline and vulnerable communities, labor unions, worker cooperatives, civil society groups, academia, and businesses; and

(4) to achieve the Green New Deal goals and mobilization, a Green New Deal will require the following goals and projects—

>(A) providing and leveraging, in a way that ensures that the public receives appropriate ownership stakes and returns on investment, adequate capital (including through community grants, public banks, and other public financing), technical expertise, supporting policies, and other forms of assistance to communities, organizations, Federal, State, and local government agencies, and businesses working on the Green New Deal mobilization;

>(B) ensuring that the Federal Government takes into account the complete environmental and social costs and impacts of emissions through—

>>(i) existing laws;

>>(ii) new policies and programs; and

(iii) ensuring that frontline and vulnerable communities shall not be adversely affected;

(C) providing resources, training, and high-quality education, including higher education, to all people of the United States, with a focus on frontline and vulnerable communities, so that all people of the United States may be full and equal participants in the Green New Deal mobilization;

(D) making public investments in the research and development of new clean and renewable energy technologies and industries;

(E) directing investments to spur economic development, deepen and diversify industry and business in local and regional economies, and build wealth and community ownership, while prioritizing high-quality job creation and economic, social, and environmental benefits in frontline and vulnerable communities, and deindustrialized communities, that may otherwise struggle with the transition away from greenhouse gas intensive industries;

(F) ensuring the use of democratic and participatory processes that are inclusive of and led by frontline and vulnerable communities and workers to plan, implement, and administer the Green New Deal mobilization at the local level;

(G) ensuring that the Green New Deal mobilization creates high-quality union jobs that pay prevailing wages, hires local workers, offers training and advancement opportunities, and guarantees wage and benefit parity for workers affected by the transition;

(H) guaranteeing a job with a family-sustaining wage, adequate family and medical leave, paid vacations, and retirement security to all people of the United States;

(I) strengthening and protecting the right of all workers to organize, unionize, and collectively bargain free of coercion, intimidation, and harassment;

(J) strengthening and enforcing labor, workplace health and safety, antidiscrimination, and wage and hour standards across all employers, industries, and sectors;

(K) enacting and enforcing trade rules, procurement standards, and border adjustments with strong labor and environmental protections—

				(i) to stop the transfer of jobs and
			pollution overseas; and
				(ii) to grow domestic manufacturing
			in the United States;
			(L) ensuring that public lands, waters, and
		oceans are protected and that eminent domain
		is not abused;
			(M) obtaining the free, prior, and informed
		consent of indigenous peoples for all decisions
		that affect indigenous peoples and their traditional territories, honoring all treaties and agreements with indigenous peoples, and protecting and enforcing the sovereignty and land rights of indigenous peoples;
			(N) ensuring a commercial environment where every businessperson is free from unfair competition and domination by domestic or international monopolies; and
			(O) providing all people of the United States with—
				(i) high-quality health care;
				(ii) affordable, safe, and adequate housing;
				(iii) economic security; and

14

1 (iv) clean water, clean air, healthy and
2 affordable food, and access to nature.

The Communist Party of America (CPUSA) Website

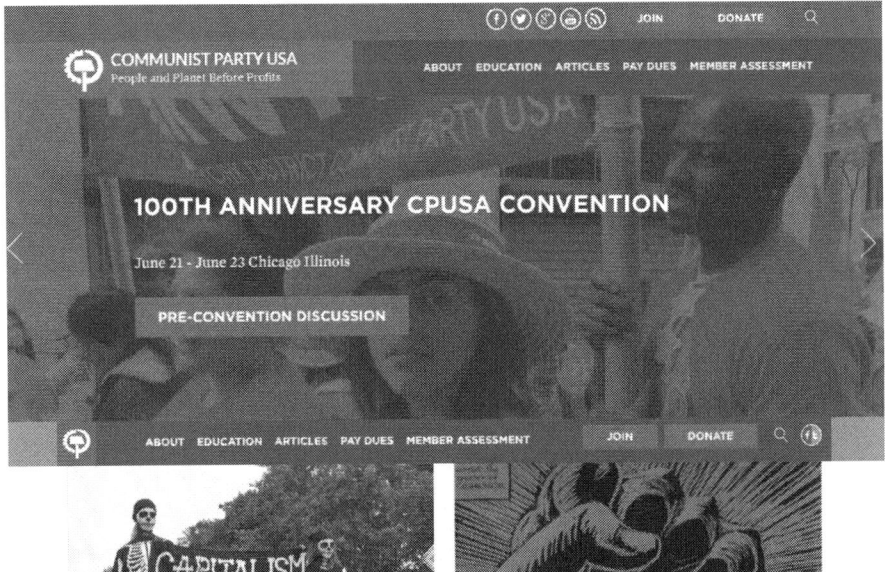

The Socialist Party of America Website

The Democratic Socialists of America (DSA) Website

DSA
Democratic Socialists of America

Home   About Us   Get Involved   Chapters   News   Resources

Who We Are & What We Do

The Democratic Socialists of America (DSA) is the largest socialist organization in the United States. We believe that working people should run both the economy and society democratically to meet human needs, not to make profits for a few. We are a political and activist organization, not a party; through campus and community based chapters, DSA members use a variety of tactics, from legislative to direct action, to fight for reforms that empower working people.

Join DSA   Donate

Current Campaigns

DSA and YDSA chapters organize around a variety of issues based on local priorities, especially labor solidarity and anti-austerity work. However, the national office provides resources and support for the main activist priorities of the organization as voted on by delegates to our national convention.

Medicare for All

Health care is a huge segment of our economy and health care access is a deeply and widely felt need. In the capitalist system, you have to pay to get care or go without, and under a democratic socialist system, we would collectively provide care as a society. Medicare for all is a stepping stone towards that vision and our campaign is designed to build a working class base of people fighting for state and national power. Click here to go to the campaign website.

Strong Unions

Capitalism pits us against each other and workplaces are fundamentally authoritarian unless workers can self-organize and build collective power. This is why people build unions, and why employers undermine them. It is also why the capitalists as a class constantly work to undermine unions and promote narratives about unions that frame them as unnecessary, undemocratic or ineffective. We are forming a national project to fight back and build power in the economy, since outside of Wall Street, workplaces are the place where the owning class extract resources from the working class. Click here to learn more about the Democratic Socialist Labor Commission.

Electoral Power

Bernie Sanders launched a political revolution and we continue to build it, supporting democratic socialist candidates running for local and state office. We're also grappling with how to build independent political power to hold candidates we elect, and others, accountable to their constituents rather than the donor class. Click here to go to our electoral website.

DSA Weekly

Upcoming Events

04/29/2019   MONDAY 8:00 PM EDT
Socialist Forum Discussion Group: Matt Huber On "Ecosocialism: Dystopian And Scientific"

📅 View all upcoming events

News and Statements

DSA Statement In Solidarity with Representative Ilhan Omar
April 15, 2019

2019 Abortion Access Bowl-a-thon: Donate or Sign Up Now!
April 8, 2019

DSA Supports the Highlander Education and Research Center. Y'allidarity.
April 2, 2019

Bernie poll results and next steps
March 19, 2019

VIEW MORE NEWS →

DSA Sites

DL DEMOCRATIC LEFT
The magazine of the Democratic Socialists of America

DSLC DEMOCRATIC SOCIALIST LABOR COMMITTEE

DSA
The main site for the Democratic Socialists of America

Open Communist Protests on the Streets of America

(Photos Courtesy of Alex Jones' InfoWars, Associated Press and Getty Images)

Author's Notes

Introduction

[1] "Antifa Mob Attacks Tucker Carlson's Home." *The Rush Limbaugh Show,* Excellence in Broadcasting Network (EIB), 8 Nov. 2018, https://www.rushlimbaugh.com/daily/2018/11/08/antifa-mob-attacks-tucker-carlsons-home/. Accessed 23 Apr. 2019.

[2] Custis, Calvin. "Antifa Mob Attack On Tucker Carlson Home labeled A 'Hate Crime' by Police." *The Federalist Papers,* FDRLST LLC, 9 Nov. 2018, https://thefederalistpapers.org/opinion/antifa-mob-attack-tucker-carlson-home-labeled-hate-crime-police. Accessed 23 Apr. 2019.

[3] "American Conservatism." *Conservapedia,* 2018, https://www.conservapedia.com/American_conservatism. Accessed 23 Apr. 2019.

[4] "Liberal." *Conservapedia,* 2019, https://www.conservapedia.com/Liberal. Accessed Apr. 2019.

[5] Kenton, Will. "Marxism." *Investopedia,* DotDash Publishing, 26 Aug. 2010, https://www.investopedia.com/terms/m/marxism.asp. Accessed 23 Apr. 2019.

[6] IBID. "Liberal".

[7] Sowell, Thomas. "Useful Idiots." *Townhall,* Salem Media, 20 May 2003, https://townhall.com/columnists/thomassowell/2003/05/20/useful-idiots-n1147831 Accessed 23 Apr. 2019.

[8] Skousen, W. Cleon. *The Naked Communist,* Verity Publishing, 1958.

[9] "Utopian Society." *The Free Dictionary.com,* 5th Edition, Houghton Miffin Harcourt Publishing, 2016, *American Heritage Dictionary of the English Language,* http://www.thefreedictionary.com/Utopian+society. Accessed 23 Apr. 2019.

[10] Madden, C. Brian. *Don't Believe the Hype!! (First Revision),* CreateSpace Independent Publishing, 2017.

[11] Griffin, G. Edward. "Former KGB Agent Yuri Bezmenov Explains How to Brainwash a Nation (FULL LENGTH)." *You Tube,* 28 Dec. 2012, https://youtu.be/5it/zarinvo. Accessed 23 Apr. 2019.

Chapter One: What is Marxism?

[1] Marx, Karl, and Friedrich Engels. *The Communist Manifesto*. Jaico Publishing House, 2018.

[2] IBID. Marx, Karl.

[3] Skousen, W. Cleon. *The Naked Communist*. Verity Publishing, 1958.

[4] Bell, Kenton. "Marxism Sociology Dictionary Definition: Marxism Defended." *Open Education Sociology Dictionary*, Open Education Sociology, 2013, http://sociologydictionary.org/marxism/. Accessed 3 Jan 2019.

[5] "Marxism." *Merriam-Webster Dictionary & Thesaurus."* Merriam-Webster Dictionary & Thesaurus, Merriam-Webster, Springfield, MA, 2007, p.293.

[6] Skousen, W. C. *The Naked Communist*. Verity Publishing, 1958.

[7] Marx, Karl, and Friedrich Engels. *The Communist Manifesto*. Jaico Publishing House, 2018.

[8] IBID. Marx, Karl and Fredrich Engels.

[9] IBID. Skousen, W. Cleon.

[10] IBID. Skousen, W. Cleon.

[11] IBID. Skousen, W. Cleon.

[12] IBID. Marx, Karl and Fredrich Engels.

Chapter Two: Who are these People?

[1] Skousen, W. Cleon. *The Naked Communist*. Verity Publishing, 1958. Pg.26-30.

[2] Marx, Karl, and Friedrich Engels. *The Communist Manifesto*. Jaico Publishing House, 2018.

[3] Bell, Kenton. "Marxism Sociology Dictionary Definition: Marxism Defended." *Open Education Sociology Dictionary*, Open Education Sociology, 2013, http://sociologydictionary.org/marxism/. Accessed 3 Jan 2019.

[4] Leopold, David. "The Young Karl Marx: German Philosophy, Modern Politics, and Human Flourishing." Cambridge UP, 2009.

[5] IBID. Skousen, W. Cleon. Pg. 37-39.

[6] IBID. Skousen, W. Cleon. Pg. 42-45.

[7] IBID. Skousen, W. Cleon. Pg. 47-52.

[8] IBID. Skousen, W. Cleon. Pg. 53-56.

[9] IBID. Skousen, W. Cleon. Pg. 57-60.

[10] IBID. Skousen, W. Cleon.

[11] IBID. Skousen, W. Cleon.

[12] IBID. Skousen, W. Cleon.

[13] IBID. Skousen, W. Cleon.

[14] Vladimir-Lenin. *Wikipedia, the Free Encyclopedia,* Wikimedia Foundation, Inc, 2019, https://en.wikipedia.org/wiki/Vladimire_Lenin. Accessed 4 Jan. 2019.

[15] Bump, Philip. "Here Is When Each Generation Begins and Ends, According to Facts." *The Atlantic*, 25 Mar. 2014.

[16] Schuman, Tomas. *World Thought Police.* NATA Almanac, 1986.

[17] Fay, Mary Jo. "Narcissism Victim Syndrome, A New Diagnosis?" *Medical News Today,* Medilexicon International, 17 July 2004, https://www.medicalnewstoday.com/articles/10872.php. Accessed 4 Jan. 2019.

[18] Orloff, Judith. "Strategies to Deal with a Victim Mentality." *Psychology Today,* Sussex Publishers LLC, 1 Oct. 2012, https://www.psychologytoday.com/blog/emotional-freedom/201210/strategies-deal-victim-mentality. Accessed 4 Jan. 2019.

[19] Pedersen, Traci. "Millennials Believe They Are the Most Narcissistic Generation." *Psych Central News,* Psych Central, 27 Mar. 2016. Https://www.psychcentral.com/news/2016/03/27/millennials-believe-

they-are-the-most-narcissistic-generation/100967.html. Accessed 4 Jan. 2019.

[20] Skousen, W. C. *The Naked Communist*. Verity Publishing, 1958.

[21] IBID. Skousen, W. Cleon.

[22] IBID. Skousen, W. Cleon.

[23] IDIB. Skousen, W. Cleon.

[24] Madden, C. Brian. "Don't Believe the Hype!! (First Revision). CreateSpace Independent Publishing, 2017.

[25] IBID. Madden, C. Brian. Pg. 41-43.

[26] IBID. Madden, C. Brian. Pg. 44-46.

[27] IBID. Madden, C. Brian. Pg. 47-49.

[28] IBID. Madden, C. Brian. Pg. 50.

[29] IBID. Madden, C. Brian. Pg. 51.

[30] "Generation X-Wikipedia." *Wikipedia, the Free Encyclopedia*, Wikimedia Foundation Inc, 2019, https://en.wikipedia.org/wiki/Generationx. Accessed 4 Jan 2019.

[31] Meglamania. "The Mentality & Personality of the Narcissist." *Experts Column*, 2017, https://www.narcissismexpertscolumn.com/article/mentality-and-personality-narcissist. Accessed 4 Jan. 2019.

[32] IBID. Meglamania.

Chapter Three: The Ideological Subversion of the United States of America

[1] Griffin, G. Edward. "Former KGB Agent Yuri Bezmenov Explains How to Brainwash a Nation (Full Length)." *You Tube*, 28 Dec. 2012, https://youtu.be/5itlzarinvo. Accessed 5 Jan. 2019.

[2] Schuman, Tomas. *World Thought Police*. NATA Almanac, 1986.

[3] IBID. Griffin, G. Edward.

[4] "Joseph Goebbels." *AZQuotes.com*, Wind and Fly LTD, 2019. https://www.azquotes.com/author/5626-Joseph_Gobbles. Accessed 28 Mar. 2019.

[5] History.com Editors. "Joseph Goebbels." *History.com,* 24 March 2010. https://www.history.com/topics/world-war-ii/joseph-goebbels. Accessed 28 Mar. 2019.

[6] "Joseph Goebbels Quotes." *BrainyQutoe.com,* Brainy Media Inc, 2019. https://www.brainyquote.com/quotes/jospeh_goebbels_401673. Accessed 28 Mar. 2019.

[7] Skousen, W. Cleon. *The Naked Communist*. Verity Publishing, 1958.

[8] Skousen, W. Cleon. *The Naked Communist*. Verity Publishing, 1958.

[9] Griffin, G. Edward. "Former KGB Agent Yuri Bezmenov Explains How to Brainwash a Nation (Full Length)." *You Tube*, 28 Dec. 2012, https://youtu.be/5itlzarinvo. Accessed 5 Jan. 2019.

[10] Schuman, Tomas. *World Thought Police*. NATA Almanac, 1986.

[11] IBID. Griffin, G. Edward.

[12] IBID. Griffin, G. Edward.

[13] IBID. Schuman, Tomas.

[14] IBID. Schuman, Tomas.

[15] IBID. Griffin, G. Edward.

[16] IBID. Schuman, Tomas.

[17] IBID. Schuman, Tomas.

[18] "Yuri Bezmenov Full Interview & Lecture-HQ." *You Tube,* 20 Mar. 2017, https://YouTu.be/pzeHpf3OYQY. Accessed 28 Mar. 2019.

[19] IBID. Yuri Bezmenov.

[20] Kengor, Paul. *The Communist*. Simon & Schuster, 2012.

[21] IBID. Kengor, Paul.

[22] IBID. Kengor, Paul.

[22] IBID. Kengor, Paul.

[23] IBID. Kengor, Paul.

[24] IBID. Kengor, Paul.

[25] IBID. Kengor, Paul.

[26] "Yuri Bezmenov Full Interview & Lecture-HQ." *You Tube,* 20 Mar. 2017, https://YouTu.be/pzeHpf3OYQY. Accessed 28 Mar. 2019.

[27] IBID. Yuri Bezmenov.

[28] IBID. Yuri Bezmenov.

[29] Madden, C. Brian. "Don't Believe the Hype!! (First Revision). CreateSpace Independent Publishing Platform, 2017.

Chapter Four: Demoralization

[1] "Yuri Bezmenov Full Interview & Lecture-HQ." *You Tube,* 20 Mar. 2017, https://YouTu.be/pzeHpf3OYQY. Accessed 28 Mar. 2019.

[2] IBID.

[3] Kengor, Paul. "The Communist". Simon & Schuster, 2012.

[4] Skousen, W. Cleon. *The Naked Communist.* Verity Publishing, 1958.

[5] Kimball, Roger. *The Long March: How the Cultural Revolution of the 1960s Changed America.* Encounter Books, 2001.

[6] "Yuri Bezmenov Full Interview & Lecture-HQ." *You Tube,* 20 Mar. 2017, https://YouTu.be/pzeHpf3OYQY. Accessed 28 Mar. 2019.

[7] Loudon, Trevor. *The Enemies Within: Communists, Socialists, and Progressives in the U.S. Congress.* Pacific Freedom Foundation, Las Vegas, NV, 2013.

[8] Brown, Susan Stamper. *Is Progressivism the New Communism.* Western Journalism, Liftable Media Inc, 24 Mar. 2017. Accessed 30 Mar. 2019.

[9] IBID. Yuri Bezmenov.

[10] Marx, Karl, and Friedrich Engels. *The Communist Manifesto.* Jaico Publishing House, 2018.

[11] IBID. Marx, Karl, and Friedrich Engels.

[12] IBID. Marx, Karl, and Friedrich Engels.

[13] "Paul Harvey." *Wikipedia, the Free Encyclopedia,* Wikimedia Foundation, Inc, 15 Jan. 2004, https://en.wikipedia.org/wiki/Paul_Harvey. Accessed 30 Mar. 2019.

[14] "If I were the Devil-(BEST VERSION) by PAUL HARVEY Audio Restored." *You Tube*, 23 Mar. 2012, http://YouTu.be/H3Az0okaHig. Accessed 30 Mar. 2019.

[15] Kimball, Roger. *Tenured Radicals: How Politics Has Corrupted Our Higher Education.* Ivan R. Dee, 2008.

[16] "Pete 'Potemkin' Seeger: Stalin's Little Minstrel." *Intellectual Conservative,* Ellis Washington, 9 Feb. 2014, https://intellecturalconservative.com/pete-potemkin-seeger-stalins-little-minstrel/. Accessed 31 Mar. 2019.

[17] "Yuri Bezmenov Full Interview & Lecture-HQ." *You Tube,* 20 Mar. 2017, https://YouTu.be/pzeHpf3OYQY. Accessed 28 Mar. 2019.

[18] Editors, Citizen Review Online. "Climate Change-Real or Imagined?" *Citizen Review Online News & Commentary,* 24 July 2014, https://citizenreviewonline.org/climate-change-real-or-imagined/. Accessed 31 Mar. 2019.

[19] Harsanyl, David. "The 10 Most Insane Requirements of the Green New Deal." *The Federalist,* FDRLST Media, 9 Feb.2019, https://thefederalist.com/2019/02/07/ten-most-insane-requirements-green-new-deal/. Accessed 31 Mar. 2019.

[20] Elliot, Tom. "The 'Green New Deal': A Radical Mandate for Government Control of American Society." *Grabien News,* 2 Jan. 2019, https://news.grabien.com/story-ocasio-cortez-green-new-deal-radical-mandate-government-com. Accessed 31 Mar. 2019.

[21] Sampson, Hedi H. "Alfred Rep. Sampson: Mandatory Cursive Lessons Will Help Maine Students Become Better Writers, Readers, Thinkers." *Portland (Maine) Press Herald,* 20 Feb. 2019, https://www.pressherald.com/2019/02/20/alfred-rep-sampson-mandatory-cursive-lessons-will-help-maine-students-become-better-writers-readers-thinkers/. Accessed 31 Mar. 2019.

[22] Editors. "Tom Purcell: Time to Embrace Cursive Handwriting Again." *Omaha.com,* https://omaha.com/opinion/tom-purcell-time-to-embrace-cursive-handwriting-again/article_0dcf03-83f2-5e48-b76c-fi86a0d37a10.html. Accessed 31 Mar. 2019.

[23] Ujifusa, Andrew. "A 'Common-Core Math' Problem: How Many States Have Adopted the Standards?" *Education Week,* State Ed Watch, Education Projects in Education, 30 June 2015. https://blogs.edweek.org/edweek/state_edwatch/2015/06/a_common_core_math_problem_how_many_states_have_adopted_the_standards.html. Accessed 2 Apr. 2019.

[24] "About the Standards." *Common Core State Standards Initiative,* https://www.corestandards.org/about-the-standards/. Accessed 2 Apr. 2019.

[25] "Antonio Gramsci." *Encyclopedia Britannica,* Encyclopedia Britannica Inc, 2019, https://www.britannica.com/biography/Antonio-Gramsci. Accessed 2 Apr. 2019.

[26] "Antonio Gramsci." *Wikipedia, the Free Encyclopedia,* Wikimedia Foundation Inc, 11 June 2002, https://en.wikipedia.org/wiki/Antonio_Gramsci. Accessed 2 April 2019.

[27] "Antonio Gramsci (1891-1937)." *Marxists Internet Archive,* 9 Jan 2001, https://www.marxists.org/archive/gramsci/index.htm. Accessed 2 Apr. 2019.

[28] Chen, James. "Homeowners Association-HOA." *Investopedia,* DotDash Publishing Company, 23 Mar. 2010. https://www.investopedia.com/terms/h/hoa.asp. Accessed 2 Apr. 2019.

[29] Murphy, Paul J. "InfoWars' Main You Tube Channel is Two Strikes Away from Being Banned." *Cable News Network (CNN),* Turner Broadcasting System, 24 Feb. 2018, https://www.cnn.com/2018/02/23/us/infowars-youtube-videos-trhd/index.html. Accessed 2 Apr. 2019.

[30] "Latest Banned Videos." *Alex Jones' InfoWars: There's a War on for Your Mind!,* Free Speech Systems LLC, 2019, https://www.inforwars.com/. Accessed 2 Apr. 2019.

[31] Skousen, W. Cleon. "The Naked Communist." Verity Publishing, 1958.

[32] Editors Citizen Review Online. "Communist Goals 1963-How Many Have Been Fulfilled." *Citizen Review Online,* Citizen Review Online LLC, 28 June 2010. http://citizenreviewonline.org/2010/jun/communism.html. Accessed 2 Apr. 2019.

[33] Starr, Penny. "1963 Congressional Record: 'Communist Goals? Include Promoting of Homosexuality as "Natural, Healthy?" *CNS News*, Media Research Center, 29 May 2015, https://www.cnsnews.com/blog/penny-star/1963-congressional-record-communist-goals-include-promoting-homosexuality-natural. Accessed 2 Apr. 2019.

[34] "Albert Syd Herlong Jr." *Wikipedia, the Free Encyclopedia,* Wikimedia Foundation Inc, 2019, https://en.wikipedia.org/wiki/syd_herlong. Accessed 2 Apr. 2019.

[35] "Spiro T. Agnew." *Encyclopedia Britannica.com,* Encyclopedia Britannica Inc, 2018, https://www.britannica.com/biography/Spiro-Agnew. Accessed 2 Apr. 2019.

[36] "Yuri Bezmenov Full Interview & Lecture-HQ." *You Tube,* 20 Mar. 2017, https://YouTu.be/pzeHpf3OYQY. Accessed 2 Apr. 2019.

[37] Madden, C. Brian. *Don't Believe the Hype!! (First Revision)*, CreateSpace Independent Publishing, 2017.

[38] IBID. Yuri Bezmenov.

[39] IBID. Yuri Bezmenov.

[40] IBID. Yuri Bezmenov.

[41] Clark, Christopher, et. al. *Who Built America?: Since 1877.* Worth Publication, 2000.

[42] Sherk, James. "$15 Minimum Wages Will Substantially Raise Prices." *The Heritage Foundation,* The Heritage Foundation, 19 Jan. 2017, https://www.heritage.org/jobs-and-labor/report/15-minimum-wages-will-substaintially-raise-prices. Accessed 2 Apr. 2019.

[43] Smith, Andrew F. *Fast Food: The Good, the Bad and the Hungry.* Reaktion Books, 2016.

[44] "Title VII, Civil Rights Act of 1964, AS AMENDED-Office of the Assistant Secretary for Administration and Management (OASM)-United States Department of Labor." *U.S. Department of Labor,* 2019, https://www.dol.gov.oasam.regs/statutes/2000-e-16.htm. Accessed 3 Apr. 2019.

[45] "The Civil Rights Act of 1964 and the Equal Employment Opportunity Commission." *National Archives,* U.S. National Archives and Records Administration, 25 April 2018, https://www.archives.gov/education/lessons/civil-raights-act. Accessed 3 Apr. 2019.

[46] "Minimum Wage Laws in the States-Wage and Hour Division (WHD)." *U.S. Department of Labor,* 2019, https://www.dol.gov/whd/america.htm#stateDetails. Accessed 3 Apr. 2019.

[47] "Wage and Hour Division (WHD)." *U.S. Department of Labor,* 2019, https://www.dol.gov/whd/flsa/. Accessed 3 Apr. 2019.

[48] "29 CFR Chapter V-Wage and Hour Division, Department of Labor." *U.S. Department of Labor*, 2019, https://wwww.dol.gov/dol/cfr/Title_29/Chapter_V.htm. Accessed 3 Apr. 2019.

[49] Chen, James. "Consumer Price Index (CPI) Definition." *Investopedia,* DotDash Publishing Company, 19 Nov. 2003, https://www.investopedia.com/terms/c/consumerpriceindex.asp. Accessed 3 Apr. 2019.

[50] "The Definition of Equality." *Dictionary.com,* Dictionary.com LLC, 2019, https://www,dictionary.com/browse.equality. Accessed 3 Apr. 2019.

Chapter Five: Destabilization

[1] Inspiring Quotes.us. "Joseph Stalin Quote: America is Like a Healthy Body and Its Resistance is Threefold: Its Patriot." *Inspiring quotes,* 2019, https://www.inspiringquotes.us/quotes/4iH5_5kVoUY40. Accessed 4 Apr. 2019.

[2] "Yuri Bezmenov Full Interview & Lecture-HQ." *You Tube,* 20 Mar. 2017, https://YouTu.be/pzeHpf3OYQY. Accessed 28 Mar. 2019.

[3] AFL-CIO. "Increasing the Minimum Wage Will Help Millions of Latino Workers." *American Unions/AFL-CICO,* 20 Mar. 2014, https://aflcio.org/reports/increasing-minimum-wage-latino-workers. Accessed 4 Apr. 2019.

[4] AFL-CIO. "New Jersey State AFL-CIO Statement on $15 An Hour Minimum Wage Law." *New Jersey State AFL-CIO,* 4 Feb. 2019, https://www.njaflcio.org/new_jersey_state_afl_cio_statement_on_15_an_hour_minimum_wage_law. Accessed 4 Apr. 2019.

[5] Greunberg, Mark. "Illinois Raises Minimum Wage to $15 Hourly By 2025." *United Steelworkers,* USWA Political Fund, 1 Mar. 2019, https://www.usw.org/blog/2019/illinois-raises-mimimum-wage-to-15-hourly-by-2025. Accessed 4 Apr. 2019.

[6] AFL-CIO. "Right to Work". *America's Unions/AFL-CIO,* 2019, https://www.aflcio.org/issues/right-to-work. Accessed 4 Apr.2019.

[7] "Right to Work Laws." *Legislative News,* Studies and Analysis/National Conference of State Legislatures, 2019, https://www.ncsl.org/research/labor-and-employment/right-to-work-laws-and-bills.aspx. Accessed 4 Apr. 2019.

[8] Condon, Stephanie. "Wisconsin Vote Spurs Death Threat, Protests, Legal Questions." *Live, Breaking News Today: Latest National News Headlines, World News, and More from CBSNews.com and Watch CBSN Live News Stream 24x7,* Columbia Broadcasting System (CBS), 10 Mar. 2011, http://www.cbsnews.com/news/wisconsin-vote-spurs-death-threat-protests-legal-questions/. Accessed 4 Apr. 2019.

[9] "Yuri Bezmenov Full Interview & Lecture-HQ." *You Tube,* 20 Mar. 2017, https://YouTu.be/pzeHpf3OYQY. Accessed 28 Mar. 2019.

[10] IBID.

[11] Yette, Samuel F. "The Threat and Tactics." *The Choice: The Issue of Black Survival in America,* G.P. Putnam's Sons, 1971. Pg. 185.

[12] "2017 Congressional Baseball Shooting." *Wikipedia, the Free Encyclopedia,* Wikimedia Foundation Inc, 14 June 2017, https://en.wikipedia.org/wiki/2017_Congressional_baseball_shooting. Accessed 4 Apr. 2019.

[13] McCausland, Phil. "It Would Have Been a Massacre: Capitol Police Officers Hailed As Heroes After Shooting." *NBC News,* National Broadcasting Company-Universal (NBC-Universal), 15 June 2017, https://www.nbcnews.com/news/us-news/capitol-police-officers-hailed-as-heroes-after-baseball-practice-shooting-n772466. Accessed 4 Apr. 2019.

[14] Silva, Daniella. "Congressman Says Shooting Suspect Asked If 'Republicans or Democrats' on the Field." *NBC News,* National Broadcasting Company-Universal (NBC-Universal), 14 June 2017, https://www.nbcnews.com/news/us-news/rep-desantis-shooting-suspect-asked-if-republicans-or-democrats-field-n772351. Accessed 4 Apr. 2019.

[15] Fox News Editors. "Scalise Critical, Shooter ID As James Hodgkinson." *Fox News,* Fox News Network LLC, 23 June 2017, https://www.foxnews.com/us/scalise-critical-shooter-idd-as-james-hodgkinson. Accessed 4 Apr. 2019.

[16] Grabien News Staff. "Left-Wing Twitter Celebrates Shooting of Rep. Scalise (UPDATED)." *Grabien News,* Grabien News, 14 June 2017, https://www.news.grabien.com/story-left-wing-celebrates-shooting-rep-scalise. Accessed 4 Apr. 2019.

[17] Newby, Joe. "Sick Liberals Hail Scalise Shooter James Hodgkinson As A Hero-Conservative Firing Line." *Conservative Firing Line,* 15 June 2017, http://conservativefiringline.com/sick-liberals-hail-scalise-shooter-james-hodgkinson-hero/. Accessed 4 Apr. 2019.

[18] Skousen, W. Cleon. "The Naked Communist." Verity Publishing, 1958.

[19] Harsanyl, David. "FISA Abuse Memo Proves the Need for an Independent Investigation." *The Federalist,* FDRLST Media, 2 Feb. 2018, https://www.thefederalist.com/2018/02/02/fisa-abuse-memo-proves-need-independent-investigation/. Accessed 5 Apr. 2019.

[20] Durden, Tom. ""Explosive", "Shocking", And "Alaming" FISA Memo Set to Rock DC, "End Mueller Investigation"." *Zero Hedge,* ABC Media LTD, 19 Jan. 2018, https://www.zerohedge.com/news/2018-01-18/explosive-shocking-and-alarming-fisa-memo-set-to-rock-dc-end-mueller-investigation. Accessed 5 Apr. 2019.

[21] Lalla, Cristina. "Here Are the 10 'Episodes' Mueller Investigated for Obstruction of Justice-Proving Mueller's Investigation Was a Farce." *The Gateway Pundit,* 19 Apr. 2019, http://www.thegatewaypundit.com/2019/04/here-are-the-10-episodes-mueller-investigated-for-obstruction-of-justice-proving-muellers-investigation-was-a-farce/. Accessed 19 Apr. 2019.

[22] Calabrese, Dan. "This Has to Stop: Liberal Federal Judge, Having No Authority to do so, Orders Keystone XL Pipeline Construction Stopped." *Herman Cain,* Western Journal, 9 Nov. 2018, https://www.westernjoural.com/hermaincain/stop-liberal-federal-judge-no-authority-orders-keystone-al-pipeline-construction-stopped/. Accessed 5 Apr. 2019.

[23] Dinan, Stephen. "Judge Blocks Trump's Wait-in-Mexico Asylum Policy." *Washington Times,* Washington Times LLC, 8 Apr. 2019, https://www.washingtontimes.com/news/2019/apr/8/judge-blocks-trump-policy-returning-asylum-seekers/. Accessed 19 Apr. 2019.

[24] ---. "Judge Tosses Travel Ban Lawsuit, Says Families Don't Have Right to Demand Visas for Relatives." *The Washington Times,* Washington Times LLC, 27 Mar. 2019, https://www.washingtontimes.com/news/2019/mar.27/judge-tosses-travel-ban-lawsuit/. Accessed 5 Apr. 2019.

[25] "Russian Collusion Hoax." *Conservapedia,* 3 Apr. 2019, https://www.conservapedia.com/Russian_collusion_hoax. Accessed 5 Apr. 2019.

[26] "The Origins of the Russian Collusion Hoax." *The Rush Limbaugh Show,* Excellence in Broadcasting Network (EIB), 5 Feb. 2018,

https://www.rushlimbaugh.com/daily/2018/02/05/the-origins-of-the-russia-collusion-hoax/. Accessed 5 Apr. 2019.

[27] Jarrett, Gregg. "Gregg Jarrett: Trump-Russia 'Collusion' Was Always a Hoax—And the Dirtiest Political Trick in Modern US History." *Fox News*, Fox News Network LLC, 25 Mar. 2019. https://www.foxnews.com/opinion/gregg-jarrett-trump-russia-collusion-was-alwasy-a-hoax-and-dirtiest-political-trick-in-modern-us-history. Accessed 5 Apr. 2019.

[28] Ross, Chuck. "Lindsey Graham Reboots FISA Abuse Investigation with Expansive DOJ Document Request." *The Daily Caller,* 7 Mar. 2019, https://www.dailycaller.com/2019/03/07/lindsey-graham-fisa-willian-barr/. Accessed 5 Apr. 2019.

[29] "Defense of Marriage Act". *Wikipedia, the Free Encyclopedia,* Wikimedia Foundation Inc, 14 Mar. 2019, https://en.wikipedia.org/wiki/Defense_of-marriage_act. Accessed 5 Apr. 2019.

[30] "Roe vs. Wade." *Findlaw,* Thomas Reuters, 2019, https://www.caselaw.findlaw.com/us-supreme-court/410/113.html. Accessed 5 Apr. 2019.

[31] Fox News Staff. "Ginsburg to Egyptians: I wouldn't Use U.S. Constitution As A Model." *Fox News,* Fox News Network LLC, 6 Feb. 2012, https://www.foxnews.com/politics/2012/02/06/ginsburg-to-egyptians-wouldn't-use-us-constitution-as-model.html. Accessed 5 Apr. 2019.

[32] Madden, C. Brian. *Don't Believe the Hype!! (First Revision).* CreateSpace Independent Publishing, 2017.

[33] Diserio, Rebecca. "BLM Leader's Damning Past Exposed After Calling for Dead Cops and Violence." *Mad World News,* Mad World News LLC, 17 July 2016, https://www.madworldnews.com/blm-leaders-damning-past/. Accessed 5 Apr. 2019.

[34] "They'd Rather Have Open Borders Than An Open Government?: McCarthy Nails Dems Over Failed Border Wall Talks." *Conservpedia,* 14 Jan. 2019, https://www.conservpedia.com/news/theyd-rather-open-borders-open-government-mccarthy-nails-dems-failed-border-wall-talks/. Accessed 5 Apr. 2019.

[35] Investors.com Editors. "Yes, Democrats Are Now the Party of Open Borders." *Investors Business Daily,* 19 July 2018, https://www.investors.com/politics/editorials/illegal-immigration-democrats-open-borders/. Accessed 5 Apr. 2019.

[36] IBID. Yuri Bezmenov.

[37] IBID. Yuri Bezmenov.

[38] IBID. Yuri Bezmenov.

[39] Jennings, Daniel G. "The Communist Party and the American Media Elite." *Free Republic,* 11 Oct. 2002, https://www.freerepublic.com/focus/news/767330/posts. Accessed 5 Apr. 2019.

[40] Kincaid, Cliff. "Communists, the Media, and the Democrat Party." *Accuracy in Media,* 5 May 2008, https://www.aim.org/aim-column/communists-the-media-and-the-democrat-party/. Accessed 5 Apr. 2019.

Chapter Six: Crisis-The American Proletariat Revolution

[1] ""ANARCHY U.S.A." 1966 John Birch Society Film (WARNING GRAPHIC)." *You Tube,* 17 Dec. 2016, https://www.youtu.be/kLqQk-jKLZg. Accessed 9 Apr. 2019.

[2] "Venezuela Timeline Chronological Timetable of Events." *World Map, World Atlas/Atlas of the World Including Facts and Flags,* World Atlas.com, 2019, https://www.worldatlas.com/webimage/countrys/samerica/venezuela/vetimeln.htm. Accessed 9 Apr. 2019.

[3] Iacob, Ivona. "Venezuela's Failed Socialist Experiment." *Forbes,* Forbes Media LLC, 24 July 2016, https://www.forbes.com/sites/ivonaiacob/2016/07/24/venezuelas-failed-socialist-experiment/#2486ade041dd. Accessed 9 Apr. 2019.

[4] "Jamie Lusinchi." *Wikipedia, the Free Encyclopedia,* Wikimedia Foundation Inc, 26 June 2004, https://en.wikipedia.org/wiki/Jaime_Lusinchi. Accessed 9 Apr. 2019.

[5] "First Presidency of Carlos Andres Perez." *Wikipedia, the Free Encyclopedia,* Wikimedia Foundation Inc, 11 Oct. 2010, https://en.wikipedia.org/wink/First_Presidency_of_Carlos_Andr%C3%A9s_P%C3%A9rez. Accessed 9 Apr. 2019.

[6] "Hugo Chavez." *Wikipedia, the Free Encyclopedia,* Wikimedia Foundation Inc, 12 Apr. 2002, https://en.wikipedia.org/wiki/Hugo_Ch%C3%A1vez. Accessed 9 Apr. 2019.

[7] Cawthorne, Andrew. "Venezuela's Chavez Re-Elected to Extend Socialist Rule." *U.S.,* Reuters, 8 Oct 2012, https://www.reuters.com/article/venezuela-election/update-12-venezuelas-chavez-re-elected-to-extend-socialist-rule-idUSL1E8L70WK20121008. Accessed 9 Apr. 2019.

[8] IBID. Iacob, Ivona.

[9] IBID. Cawthorne, Andrew.

[10] IBID. "Hugo Chavez".

[11] "We're Organizing for Action." *Organizing for Action (OFA),* 2019, https://www.ofa.us/about/. Accessed 11 Apr. 2019.

[12] Berman, Ari. "Jim Messina, Obama's Enforcer." *The Nation,* The Nation Company LLC, 29 June 2015, http://www.nation.com/article/jim-messina-obamas-enforcer. Accessed 11 Apr. 2019.

[13] Thrush, Glenn, et. al. "Obama Unveils 'Organizing for Action'". *Politico,* Politico LLC, 17 Jan. 2013, https://www.politico.com/story/2013/01/obama-campaign-to-relaunch-as-tax-exempt-group-086375. Accessed 11 Apr. 2019.

[14] IBID. Iacob, Ivona.

[15] IBID. "Hugo Chavez".

[16] IBID. "Venezuela Timeline Chronological Timetable of Events."

[17] IBID. "Hugo Chavez".

[18] Weisbot, Mark, et. al. *The Chavez Administration at 10 Years: The Economy and Social Indicators,* Center for Economic and Policy Research, 2009, https://cepr.net/documents/publications/venezuela-2009-02.pdf. Accessed 11 Apr. 2019.

[19] Devereaux, Charlie, and Daniel Cancel. "Chavez Activates Price Law to End Capitalist Speculation." *Bloomberg,* Bloomberg LP, 22 Nov. 2011, https://www.bloomberg.com/news/2011-11-22/chavez-activates-price-law-to-end-capitalist-speculation-1-.html. Accessed 11 Apr. 2019.

[20] Castillo, Marino, and Osmary Hernandez. "Hugo Chavez, Influential Leader with Mixed Record, Dies at 58." *Cable News Network (CNN),* Turner Broadcasting System, 6 Mar. 2013, https://www.cnn.com/2013/03/05/world/americas/obit-venezuela-chavez/index.html. Accessed 11 Apr. 2019.

[21] Cawthorne, Andrew, and Daniel Wallace. "Venezuela's Hugo Chavez Dies from Cancer." *U.S. Reuters,* Reuters, 5 Mar. 2013, https://www.reuters.com/articles/us-venezuela-chavez/venezuela-hugo-chavez-dies-from-cancer-idUSBRE92405420130305. Accessed 11 Apr. 2019.

[22] Keppel, Stephen. "5 Ways Chavez Has Hurt the Venezuelan Economy." *Fusion,* American Broadcasting Company (ABC) News Network, 25 Oct. 2013,

http://web.archive.org/web/20140919223723/fusion.net/abc_univsion/news/story/ways-chavez-destoryed-venezuelan-economy-16104. Accessed 11 Apr. 2019.

[23] "Nicola Maduro." *Wikipedia, the Free Encyclopedia,* Wikimedia Foundation Inc, 26 Sep. 2006, https://en.wikipedia.org/wiki/Nicol%C3%A1s_Maduro. Accessed 9 Apr. 2019.

[24] Wallenfeldt, Jeff. "Nicolas Maduro: Biography, Facts & Presidency." *Encyclopedia Britannica,* Encyclopedia Britannica Inc, 2019, https://www.britannica.com/biography/Nicolas-Maduro. Accessed 11 Apr. 2019.

[25] *Crackdown on Dissent.* Human Rights Watch, 29 Nov. 2017, https://www.hrw.org/report/2017/11/29/crackdown-dissent/brutality-torture-and-political-persecution-venezuela. Accessed 11 Apr. 2019.

[26] Grillo, Ioan, and Jorge Benezra. "Inside the Hell of Venezuelan Police Prisons." *Time,* Time USA LLC, 8 June 2016, https://time.com/4360758/inside-the-hell-of-venezuelan-police-prisons/. Accessed 11 Apr. 2019.

[27] "Venezuela's Humanitarian Emergency: Large-Scale UN Response Needed to Address Health and Food Crisis." *Human Rights Watch,* 4 Apr. 2019, https://www.hrw.org/report/2019/04/04/venezuelas-humanitarian-emergency/large-scale-un-response-needed-address-health. Accessed 11 Apr. 2019.

[28] "Venezuela's Humanitarian Crisis: Severe Medical and Food Shortages, Inadequate and Repressive Government Response." *Human Rights Watch,* 24 Oct. 2016, https://www.hrw.org/report/2016/10/24/venezuelas-humanitarian-crisis/severe-medical0and-food-shortages-inadequate-and. Accessed 11 Apr. 2019.

[29] Worstall, Tim. "Venezuela's Starving People Are Now Eating Zoo Animals-The Parisians Had the German Excuse." *Forbes,* Forbes Media LLC, 17 Aug. 2017, https://www.forbes.com/sites/timworshall/2017/08/17/venezuelas-starving-people-are-now-eating-the-zoo-animals-the-partisans-had-the-german-excuse/#16a46e67dscc. Accessed 11 Apr. 2019.

[30] Martell, Frances. "Venezuelans Eating Dogs, Zoo Animals as Economy Collapses." *Breitbart,* 5 Sep. 2017, https://www.breitbart.com/national-security/2017/09/05/venezuelans-eating-dogs-zoo-animals/. Accessed 11 Apr. 2019.

[31] "Hugo Chavez." *Wikipedia, the Free Encyclopedia,* Wikimedia Foundation Inc, 12 Apr. 2002, https://en.wikipedia.org/wiki/Hugo_Ch%C3%Alvez. Accessed 9 Apr. 2019.

[32] "List of Obama's Czars." *Glenn Beck,* Mercury Radio Arts, 7 May 2018, https://www.glennbeck.com/content/articles/article/198/29391/. Accessed 12 Apr. 2019.

[33] Fox News Editors. "List of Obama Administration 'Czars'". *Fox News,* Fox News Network LLC, 22 Jan. 2015, https://www.foxnews.com/politics/list-of-obama-administration-czars. Accessed 12 Apr. 2019.

[34] "List of U.S. Executive Branch Czars." *Wikipedia, the Free Encyclopedia,* Wikimedia Foundation Inc, 4 July 2009, https://en.wikipedia.org/wiki/List_of_U.S._executive-branch-czars. Accessed 12 Apr. 2019.

[35] "Yuri Bezmenov Full Interview & Lecture-HQ." *You Tube,* 20 Mar. 2017, https://YouTu.be/pzeHph3OYQY. Accessed 12 Apr. 2019.

[36] *What is Sharia Law,* Law Library of Congress, 2015, https://www.loc.gov/law/help/sharia-law.php Accessed 12 Apr. 2019.

[37] IBID. Yuri Bezmenov Full Interview & Lecture-HQ."

[38] Bryum, Sunnivie. "The True Meaning of the Word 'Cisgender'." *Gay News, LGBT Rights, Politics, Entertainment,* The Advocate, 31 July 2015, http://www.advocate.com/transgender/2015/07/13/true-meaning-word-cisgender. Accessed 12 Apr. 2019.

[39] Steinmetz, Katy. "This IS What 'Cisgender' Means." *Time,* Time USA LLC, 23 Dec 2014, http://time.com/3636430/cisgender-definition/. Accessed 12 Apr. 2019.

[40] Issac, Cheryl. "What Reality TV Is Doing to Women." *Forbes,* Forbes Media LLC, 16 May 2012, http://www.forbes.com/sites/worldviews/2012/04/20/what-reality-tv-is-doing-to-women/#a4ccbb542774. Accessed 12 Apr. 2019.

[41] Flynn, Mark. "Reality TV and Body Image: The Not So Real World." *Behavioral Scientist,* The Psych Report, 24 June 2015, http://www.thepsychreport.com/science/reality-tv-and-body-image-the-not-so-real-world/. Accessed 12 Apr. 2019.

[42] White, Jamie. "Report: UN, Soros Behind Migrant Caravan Invasion." *Alex Jones' InfoWars: There's a War on for your Mind!,* Free Speech Systems LLC, 21 Oct. 2018, https://www.infowars.com/report-un-soros-behind-migrant-caravan-invasion/. Accessed 12 Apr. 2019.

[43] Rodrigez, Rafael. "UN Agency Assists Central American Caravan Migrants, Voices Concern for Receiving Countries." *UN News,* 6 Nov. 2018, https://news.un.org/en/story/2018/11/1024882. Accessed 12 Apr. 2019.

[44] Sleiman, Dana. "UN Refugee Chief Urges Security Council for Firm Response to Record-High Displacement." *UNHCR,* 9 Apr. 2019, https://www.unhcr.org/en-us/news/latest/2019/4/5/cad10c74/un-refugee-chief-urges-security-council-firm-response-record-high-displacement.html. Accessed 12 Apr. 2019.

[45] "What is DACA?". *UNDOCUMENTED STUDENT PROGRAM,* University of California-Berkeley, 10 Apr. 2019, https://undocu.berkely.edu/legal-support-overview/what-is-daca/. Accessed 12 Apr. 2019.

[46] *Deferred Action for Childhood Arrivals (DACA) and Deferred Action for Parents of Americans and Lawful Permanent Residents (DAPA),* U.S. Immigration Customs and Immigration Enforcement, 24 July 2018. https://www.ice.gov/daca. Accessed 12 Apr. 2019.

[47] Alex Jones Show. "Open Borders: Cartels Funding Deep State Operations in America." *Alex Jones' InfoWars: There's a War on for your Mind!",* Free Speech Systems LLC, 12 Jan. 2019, https://www.inforwars.com/open-borders-cartels-funding-deep-state-operations-in-america/. Accessed 12 Apr. 2019.

[48] Reese, Greg. "Open Borders, National Sovereignty and Common Sense." *Alex Jones' InforWars: There's a War on for your Mind!".,* Free Speech Systems LLC, 11 Jan. 2019, https://www.infowars.com/open-borders-national-sovereignty-and-common-sense/. Accessed 12 Apr. 2019.

[49] Pollak, Joel B. "How the Left Misinterprets the Bible to Promote Open Borders." *Breitbart,* 19 June 2018, https://www.breitbart.com/politics/2018/06/19/pollak-how-the-left-interprests-the-bible-to-promote-open-borders/#. Accessed 12 Apr. 2019.

[50] Colby, Sandra L., Jennifer M. Ortman. *Projections of the Size and Composition of the U.S.: 2014-2060.* U.S. Census Bureau, 3 Mar. 2015, https://www.census.gov/library/publications/2015/demo/p25-1143.html. Accessed 12 Apr. 2019.

[51] "Sanctuary City." *Conservapedia,* 2019, http://www.conservapedia.com/Sanctuary_city. Accessed 12 Apr. 2019.

[52] Hickey, Jennifer G. "More Cities Offering to Pay Legal Defense for Illegal Immigrants." *Fox News,* Fox News Network LLC, 5 May 2017, https://www.foxnews.com/politics/more-cities-offereing-to-pay-legal-defense-for-illegal-immigrants. Accessed 12 Apr. 2019.

[53] Dinan, Stephen. "California Sanctuary Policies Prompt Manslaughter, Rape Convicts' Release." *The Washington Times,* Washington Times LLC, 14 June 2018, https://www.washingtontimes.com/news/2018/jun/14/california-sanctuary-policies-prompt-manslaughter-/. Accessed 12 Apr. 2019.

[54] ---, and Gabriella Munoz. "Donald Trump Says He's Looking to Ship Illegal Immigrants to Sanctuary Cities." *The Washington Times,* Washington Times LLC, 12 Apr. 2019, https://www.washingtontimes.com/news/2019/apr/12/trump-looking-illegal-immigrants-sanctuary-cities/?fbclid=IwAR0zvB6ntfHDCIZdkET_qFC7nJKJ4cUTcv_FwU5CGuVcSFueDCWtjBi8Ajc. Accessed 12 Apr. 2019.

Chapter Seven: Normalization-The United Soviet States of America (USSA)

[1] Griffin, G. Edward. "Former KGB Agent Yuri Bezmenov Explains How to Brainwash a Nation (FULL LENGTH)." *YouTube,* 28 Dec. 2012, https://youtu.be/5itzarinvo. Accessed 12 Apr. 2019.

[2] Shuman, Tomas. *World Thought Police,* NATA Almanac, 1986.

[3] "Yuri Bezmenov Full Interview & Lecture-HQ." *YouTube,* 20 Mar. 2017, https://youtu.be/pzeHpfOYQY. Accessed 12 Apr. 2019.

[4] IBID. Griffin, Edward G.

[5] Skousen, W. Cleon. *The Naked Communist,* Verity Publishing, 1958.

[6] IBID. Skousen, W. Cleon.

[7] IBID. Skousen, W. Cleon.

[8] IBID. Skousen, W. Cleon.

[9] Schuman, Tomas. *Love Letter to America,* NATA Almanac, 1984.

[10] IBID. Schuman, Tomas.

[11] IBID. Schuman, Tomas.

[12] "FREEDOM DENIED: Cuba's Black Spring Continues." *YouTube,* The Freedom Collection, 16 July 2015, https://youtu.be/9sHbUVhsOP4. Accessed 16 Apr. 2019.

[13] "Entrevista Armando Valladares." *YouTube*, The Freedom Collection, 13 Jan 2014, https://youtu.be/14DD0eckmmo. Accessed 16 Apr. 2019.

[14] "Gulag: History, Camps, Conditions, Economy, Effect, Facts, Quotes (2003)". *YouTube,* 13 Aug. 2016, https://youtu.be/aGeHPwgLm6y. Accessed 16 Apr. 2019.

[15] "FEMA Camps Conspiracy Theory." *Wikipedia, the Free Encyclopedia,* Wikimedia Foundation Inc, 2019. https://en.wikipedia.org/wiki/FEMA_campus_conspiracy_theory. Accessed 16 Apr. 2019.

[16] "FEMA DEATH CAMPS." *Know the Real Truth,* Wordpress, 9 June 2018, http://choosethetruth.wordpress.com/2018/06/09/fema-death-camps/. Accessed 16 Apr. 2019.

[17] IBID. "FEMA DEATH CAMPS."

[18] IBID. "FEMA DEATH CAMPS."

[19] Nimmo, Kurt, and Alex Jones. "Exclusive: Government Activating FEMA Camps Across U.S." *Alex Jones InfoWars: There's a War on for your Mind!,* Free Speech Systems LLC, 7 Dec 2011.

[20] "Justice Scalia: Americans Will Be Detained in FEMA Camps." *Truth and Action,* 16 Feb. 2016, http://www.truthandaction.org/justice-scalia-americans-could-be-detained-fema-camps/2/. Accessed 16 Apr. 2019.

[21] American Patriot Editors. "AMERICAN CONCENTRATION CAMPS." *APFN,* American Patriots Friends Network, http://www.apfn.org/apfn/camps.htm. Accessed 16 Apr. 2019.

[22] IBID. American Patriot Editors.

[23] "18 Cuban Dissidents Offer New Agenda for the Transition." *Miami-Herald,* 11 Apr. 2008, https://www.miamiherald.com/latest-news/article1929132.html. Accessed 16 Arp. 2019.

[24] Tamayo, Juan O., Nora G. Torres. "Prison, Death, Exile: Outcomes of Peaceful Opposition to a Communist Cuba." *Miami-Herald,* 26 Nov 2016, https://www.miamiherald.com/news/nation-world/world/americas/fidel-castro-en/article117201468.html.

[25] Skousen, W. Cleon. *The Naked Communist,* Verity Publishing, 1958.

[26] "Russian Famine of 1921-22." *Wikipedia, the Free Encyclopedia,* Wikimedia Foundation Inc, 2019, https://en.wikipedia.org/wiki/Russian_famine_of_1921%e2%80%9322. Accessed 16 Apr. 2019.

[27] Kenan, George F. *Russia and The West Under Lenin and Stalin,* Boston UP, 1961.

[28] Yakovlev, Alexander N., et al. *A Century of Violence in Soviet Russia*, Yale UP, 2004.

[29] Edwards, Lee. "The Legacy of Mao Zedong is Mass Murder." *The Heritage Foundation,* 2 Feb. 2010, https://www.heritage.org/asia/commentary/the-legacy-mao-zedong-mass-murder. Accessed 23 Apr. 2019.

[30] Editors of Encyclopedia Britannica. "Maoism." *Encyclopedia Britannica,* 2018, https://www.britannica.com/topic/Maoism. Accessed 23 Apr. 2019.

[31] Fitzgerald, Andrew. "10 Terrible Famines In History." *Listverse,* Listverse LTD, 20 June 2014, https://listverse.com/2013/04/10/10-terrible-famines-in-history/. Accessed 23 Apr. 2019.

[32] Hasell, Joe, and Max Roser. "Famines." *Our World In Data,* Oxford UP, 12 Dec. 2017, https://www.ourworldindata.org/famines. Accessed 23 Apr. 2019.

[33] "Ronald Reagan Quotes." *BrianyQuote,* 16 Apr. 2019, http://www.brainyquote.com/quotes/ronald_reagan_183965. Accessed 23 Apr. 2019.

Made in the USA
Columbia, SC
29 October 2020